FIND ING MY WILD

'A heartbeat of a book ... that will speak to so many.'
Ruth Fitzmaurice, author of *I Found My Tribe*

'An honest but beautiful account of losing yourself through life's
tragedies and finding yourself again in the wilds of
your beloved homeland.'
Niamh Fitzpatrick, author of *Tell Me the Truth About Loss*

'There is magic in this book. With her deep-rooted attachment to the
natural world and keen observation of its rhythms, Kathy Donaghy
shares her cache of wisdom about a pared-back life enriched by
the countryside's treasure trove. Her beautifully told chronicle is a
testament to outcomes transformed by a leap of faith.'
Martina Devlin, columnist and novelist

Kathy Donaghy is an award-winning journalist, who works as a freelance writer for the *Irish Independent*. Working as a journalist for almost thirty years, she was on the staff of the *Irish Independent* and RTÉ.

After many years in Dublin, she returned home to the Inishowen Peninsula in County Donegal, where she grew up. She began writing this book at a friend's windswept cottage at Malin Head when this story, her own, kept calling her to the wild places to speak her truth.

She lives in Inishowen with her husband, the journalist, broadcaster and author Richard Curran, and their two sons, Dallan and Oirghiall.

When she's not writing, she can be found swimming in the sea or exploring the wilderness of County Donegal with her collie, Wyatt.

FINDING MY WILD

How a Move to the Edge Brought Me Home

KATHY DONAGHY

THE O'BRIEN PRESS
DUBLIN

First published 2023 by The O'Brien Press Ltd,
12 Terenure Road East, Rathgar, Dublin 6, D06 HD27, Ireland.
Tel: +353 1 4923333; Fax: +353 1 4922777
E-mail: books@obrien.ie
Website: obrien.ie
The O'Brien Press is a member of Publishing Ireland.

ISBN: 978-1-78849-356-7

10 9 8 7 6 5 4 3 2 1
28 27 26 25 24 23

Book cover design and book design: Emma Byrne. Image courtesy of Shutterstock.
Back photograph: Lorcan Doherty, with kind permission of Independent newspapers.

Printed and bound by Scandbook AB, Sweden.
The paper in this book is produced using pulp from managed forests.

Published in:

For Richard, Dallan and Oirghiall.

Acknowledgements

Thanks to Richard, Dallan and Oirghiall for their love and support. Thanks to my parents, Terence and Philomena, and my sisters, Anne-Marie and Carol, for always believing in me.

Thanks to all the extended Curran family and especially my sister-in-law Margaret and her partner, Patrick. You are both kindness personified.

Thanks to my wonderful and eclectic bunch of friends – you know who you are – thanks for the swims, coffees and chats that kept me buoyed up when I lost confidence. Thanks to my friend Jackie Doherty, who kindly let me stay in her house at Malin Head where I wrote this book.

Thanks to my various editors at the *Irish Independent* for their support, especially Tom Coogan, Yvonne Hogan, Bairbre Power and Rachel Dugan.

Thanks to everyone at the O'Brien Press, especially to my editor Susan Houlden for her unwavering patience and gentle guidance through the writing of this book, and to Emma Byrne, who designed the cover.

I would also like to acknowledge Michael O'Brien, who championed this book, and whose words of encouragement I will never forget. I only wish he were here to see *Finding My Wild* out in the world, where he wanted it.

Finally, I'd like to acknowledge and honour the place that inspired so much of this book, the magical place that is Inishowen – home.

CONTENTS

MY DREAM

There is a dream that comes regularly to me. In it, I'm running. I must be ten years old and I've hopped the ditch and climbed over the barbed-wire fence into the field in front of my parents' house. I run past the sheep grazing nearby and leap over the stone wall at the far end of the field. I keep running, further and further. I am far from home now. In the distance, the standing stone we call the druid's altar rises up against the expanse of empty field around it. I come here sometimes to run and to play, to imagine a time when ancient people worshipped at this place. I'm running so fast I'm out of breath. The wind whips up and makes me giddy. I have nowhere to go and nowhere to be. I am completely and resolutely happy in my own skin; this wild girl who is never happier than when she's discovering some secret spot where a bird might have laid a bright blue egg in a secret ditch. I lost her for a while. Life in all its ups and downs stole her away. But I got her back. This is the story of how.

CHAPTER 1

A childhood home

What was it about *this* place that wouldn't let me go?
I'd feel its tug when the wind blew in from the sea;
the compass settings of my heart pulling me true north
to a place where the gulls' cries were as familiar as the voices
of old friends, and the evening light on Lough Foyle looked
like underwater stars.

I'm not in my youth anymore but standing on this shore, so familiar to me, I often think I haven't moved too far from that girl I once was. So many years have passed since I first played here among the bladderwrack, terns and abandoned boats. So much has changed and yet when I think of my changes – my own metamorphosis from girl to woman – I think they happened right here in this place, on this small stretch of beach beside my home.

I've thought about home a lot, about what it is and what it means these past few years. Place and people, community, a physical structure where you close the door behind you and exhale. But it's also in yourself; you carry it in the chambers of your heart and sometimes you forget that the home you offer yourself is the most important place of all. I forgot that and I got lost and it took me a while to come back because home is ultimately yourself.

Of course home is also a place of comfort and knowing in the deepest folds of yourself that you belong somewhere. Maybe it's about family – the one you were born into or the one you choose. For me it's all those things too but it's also about rootedness in place. My place is Donegal, the outer reaches of it – on the Inishowen Peninsula.

Why am I telling you all this? Why do I want to begin with an exploration of home, to invite you into the private spaces and places in my life that make me, me? I've thought long and hard about this and I'm afraid to tell these truths and afraid not to in equal measure. I've been a journalist, telling people's stories for the best part of thirty years. I've asked people to share the best and worst things in life that ever happened to them. I have thought about putting into writing some of my own worst and best and then scrapped the idea thinking, 'Get a grip, who'd be interested?'

The truth is that this is the story that kept bubbling up. I've wanted to write a book since I could hold a pencil. I didn't think this would be the one I'd write. I imagined a novel. But this story, my own story, wouldn't let me go. When I talked to friends about life, about the things in our lives that shaped us and I told them some of the things I've made sense of over the years, they universally responded that I needed to write these things down. I fought hard against it. Are there not enough memoirs in the world? I don't even know if what I'm presenting to you in these pages is a memoir. I hope it's a record of a time in my life, some lessons learned along the way. I could never hope to write a self-help book and this certainly isn't that. I hope this is, more than anything else, a testament to love. At the end of the day, that's really all that matters. It's all that will be left of us in the end so it's why I'm starting at the beginning and my love affair with place, my homeplace. And the beginning for me is in Inishowen, the place that juts out into the sea at the northernmost tip of Ireland.

Surrounded by water, it's almost an island. Standing atop Sliabh Sneacht, its tallest mountain, you can see why it's called Ireland in miniature, with Lough Swilly on one side, Lough Foyle on the other and the big blue Atlantic

Ocean swirling at its headlands. I drank deeply of it as a child. A wild place like this never leaves your soul – it informs how you see the world no matter how far you travel. The blue spaces in my life created room for my imagination to grow. The green spaces allowed me freedom to roam and explore.

The place we're from never really leaves us. It's carved in our souls. Donegal left an indelible mark on mine. I compared other places to it. A lot of times they fell short. Over the course of the many years I didn't live in Donegal, I would dream about it. In the dreams I'd visit my favourite childhood haunts: abandoned cottages, glens with rushing streams or the shores of Lough Foyle, where I spent much of my time growing up.

Often I would wake from a dream, confused that I was in my bed a long way from Donegal. I had, only seconds earlier, been standing on my shore, playing in the sand or climbing into my father's cot, the little boat he'd row out to his larger fishing boat moored in deeper water.

This shore felt like my kingdom. I ruled this little stretch of rough sand with my bucket and spade. It never ceased to amaze me. I dug for sand eels, looked for buried treasure, gathered sea glass and watched the comings and goings of the gulls, the herons and the cormorants. I walked barefoot in the spirulina and across the muddy sediment at the water's edge we called the glar. So much of my dreaming and changes were here on this beach, right beside where I live once again. Even when I was far away, the constant ebb and flow of Lough Foyle in my life was always there. It felt like the rhythm of my heart.

My little shore is not the most beautiful stretch of coastline in the world. Very few people walk along it, preferring to go for the more dramatic swathes of the Atlantic Ocean. But the shore at Redcastle, which was right across the road from my primary school and a stone's throw from my father's family homestead, has always been a place of quiet beauty for me. It's home to terns and sanderlings, who move as a tight pack when you get too close, their tiny legs working frantically in unison away from you before launching into flight as one. There are always herons proudly and quietly standing guard, looking out to the horizon. In the winter, the Brent geese come to us from the north-east of Canada, walking the tideline, picking up vegetation and seaweed. If you stray too close, the one nearest to shore will emit a short, gruff warning to its family members and off they'll all swim.

All around my parents' house were big open fields that I loved to explore. Climbing walls and ditches, I'd walk for miles, straying to the outer limits of my childhood. In some of these fields, the walls of old stone houses stood and I'd play here for a while, making up new worlds of my own. When I got my first bike, I'd explore a bit further, often dragging my younger sister Anne-Marie with me to find a new place to play and convert into our own kingdom. There was a large rock in the field behind my parents' house where I loved to sit and dream. It was the perfect place to watch the sun go down over Lough Foyle. I imagined people in distant places living busy lives far from mine in this quiet spot and even though I loved it here, there was always a pull, a curiosity about other places.

And so, like many other young people from country areas, I left home to go to university when I was seventeen. After college I made a new life in Dublin. Sometimes in the middle of that new life as a journalist for a national newspaper, I'd find myself walking across O'Connell Bridge in the heart of the city, cup of coffee in hand, suited and booted and on my way back from a press conference. And for a split second, as I crossed the wide expanse of the city's widest bridge, I'd get a scent of the sea. I would tilt my head and close my eyes and breathe that old familiar scent. It was the Liffey, but in that moment, I was back at home along the shore, where the world moved at a slower pace. It would stop me in my tracks, the feeling pulling me in a different direction, before I would carry on with my busy life. Inishowen was a different world away, one I'd left behind but could never forget.

My people have been rooted in Inishowen for generations. My father Terence's family, the Smyths, lived in the townland of Ballyargus near the village of Redcastle. My great-grandfather built a traditional two-room stone cottage where he reared his nine children. Most of them emigrated or moved away. My father's aunt Maggie and his uncle Jim were like grandparents to my sisters and me growing up. Jim lived in the old Smyth homestead, while Maggie built her two-bedroom house at the opposite end of the shingle lane in the late 1950s.

My mother Philomena's family were farmers from the townland of Ballymacarthur in Greencastle. My grandfather died when I was five years old and my memories of him are scant but my maternal grandmother, Kathleen, was a formidable woman, a brilliant farmer who could grow anything.

We spent almost every Saturday of childhood with her, my younger sister Anne-Marie and I. My youngest sister, Carol, wasn't born till many years later and by that time my grandmother had left the farm. Her home was a beautiful windswept place with a bird's-eye view of Lough Foyle opening up into the wide mouth of the Atlantic. We helped her milk the goats, feed the hens and tend the horse. My first memories of picking bilberries is along the Glen Road that leads right to Kinnagoe Bay where the Atlantic's rolling waves almost always look like giants, whatever the weather. We spent hours in the summer months picking the ripe berries, which grow on dense bushes low to the ground.

The sea has featured strongly in all of the stories and lore of my family. *La Trinidad Valencera*, one of the Spanish Armada ships, foundered at Kinnagoe Bay. My grandparents' house was only a few miles from the bay and it's always been said that the Spanish sailors who survived settled in the townlands nearby. I don't know if it's true but many members of my mother's family were what are known as the 'black Irish', Irish people whose dark looks could mean they could pass off as Spaniards. I look like that too.

On my father's side, the sea was life itself. His family had held the first salmon-fishing licences on Lough Foyle. They were talented salmon fishermen. Nets were everywhere when we were growing up, hanging out to dry in sheds or strewn out on grass where the crabs and shells had to be picked out of them. Stories abounded of hungry seals with sharp teeth stealing their precious catch. Seals were always the enemy, which feels strange as I adore these beautiful creatures and love nothing more than when they pop their heads up out of the sea when I'm swimming.

According to the legend of Fionn Mac Cumhail, the salmon was a mythical creature which held the wisdom of the world. In our family salmon were indeed revered.

They represented bounty and plenty and my mother would reverently fillet them and fry the darnes in the pan with butter. When my father stopped fishing, he would often get a gift of a whole salmon from one of the other fishermen during the salmon-fishing season, a tradition long since ended. The gift of a whole salmon was holy in its own way, acknowledging the heritage and tradition of place and my own family's part in it. I can still picture the present of a large full salmon wrapped in newspaper and all that represented. This was indeed a precious gift.

When I was very young, my father found himself in the middle of a storm while out fishing on the Foyle during the salmon season. It is called Lough Foyle but it's really an inlet of the Atlantic Ocean and can be extremely rough in bad weather. I remember the candle lit in the window and my mother keeping watch. He came home safely to us that night, but the power of the sea and its need to be respected were feelings I innately understood from a young age.

Legend has it that the mouth of the Atlantic, where Lough Foyle flows into the ocean near Greencastle, is also the home of the sea god, Mannanán Mac Lir. He lived on the tuns – sandbanks that appear between Magilligan Point and Inishtrahull Island. You can see them on stormy days when the white horses ride roughshod over them. Locals believe that Mannanán's spirit is released during fierce storms and the tuns are said to be the entrance to his kingdom, where his chariot *Wave-sweeper* is led by his fierce steed Énbarr of the flowing mane.

These stories of myth and legend infused my childhood. When I was growing up, the first thing I saw when I looked out the window each morning was the Foyle. Last thing at night, I saw it too, with the full moon reflected on its surface and the familiar buoys lit up for passing ships that you could sometimes hear as they powered along.

In the summers of my childhood, the extended Smyth family would come home to the family homestead in Ballyargus from Glasgow, London and Dublin. Brothers and sisters would set up deckchairs outside my great-aunt Maggie's house and talk and talk, but not before they had walked the shore and bathed their feet in the healing properties of the seaweed. This was a sacred space and it was understood that to walk barefoot there was a necessary ritual of homecoming. It's one I have adopted whenever I leave home, even for a few days. I feel the pull of the sea and need to dip my feet in the waters of the Foyle to ground and root me back home again.

The sea ran deep in all our lives as a powerful force of giving and taking. While it provided a living, it also brought loved ones away from home. There was no other option for so many of my father's family but to leave. When I was a girl, my great-uncle Con, who emigrated to Glasgow, told me the story of the Maiden Rock, a rock that sits at the edge of Redcastle Shore. It's grassy on top and spacious enough for several people to sit and have a picnic there.

When he was young, it was the place where locals lit fires for departing emigrants. They did this so the last thing their loved ones would see, as they left home on passenger ships taking them off to new lives, would be the fires of home burning brightly for them and lighting the way. Con's stories – for he was the keeper of all our family's tales – captivated me. He never tired of telling me stories about our place and its people and I never tired of listening to them.

My great-uncle Jim was a man of few words. He carried wheelbarrow loads of seaweed across the road from the shore to fertilise his potatoes. I can still see him pushing the barrow full of bladderwrack up the lane, the whiff of it pungent as he rolled it past. Jim had a way of knowing what the weather would be like just by looking at the sky over the water and the movement of birds. I am trying to learn this skill. As each year goes past and I observe the movements of birds, I feel I understand more about how all of nature is intertwined, although the wild creatures know this more innately than we do.

Behind the house where my great-aunt and uncle lived is a small wood. It's full of silver birch trees, numerous oak trees, holly trees and giant sycamores. In the summer the bilberry bushes are laden with fruit. In the winter the holly trees bloom with waxy leaves and bright red berries. Throughout my childhood, if I wasn't at the shore, I was in the woods. I spent almost as much time at my great-uncle and aunt's place as I did at home with my parents in the neighbouring townland of Drung. My mother would often sigh and suggest that some day my rough edges might be worn down smooth as she repaired yet another piece of clothing shredded by briars after I'd run through the woods.

On hot summer's days, the woods were the perfect place to cool off. The velvety green moss underfoot felt refreshing, the trees sheltering me from the sun. I saw them as sentries to my family's history and strong upright guardians of our place. It would have been hard not to fall in love with this place, and I did.

As children we often stayed overnight at weekends with Maggie in the house next door to Jim's. I have a memory of looking out the window as Jim stepped outside his house before going to bed. I couldn't see his face but his outline was lit up from behind by the light of his living room. He glanced up at the sky. It was a practice I observed him make on a few occasions. My younger self would watch and wonder what it was like to go to bed in the same place every night without ever having gone much further than the end of the lane. I didn't want to be like that. I wanted to see the world, to travel and follow my dreams, dreams that often seemed too big for me.

Now I think back to that memory and wonder who had it right. Jim was satisfied with his world, sure of his place in it. It made him happy to step outside at night and watch as the moon waxed and waned over his beloved Foyle. I have developed the same habit of stepping outside my own front door at night, taking in the same ancient view as he did. I'm older now. My wanderlust has been calmed. The storm that raged in me to wander far from home has given way to a calm sea inside. Now I always want to see the stars and the moon over Lough Foyle before I go to sleep too. I realise that perhaps I had to go away to appreciate my homeplace. I realise too that my choices led me here, back to this place that is my home. With the benefit of hindsight, I see that I was always going to find my way back. I don't think I could have done otherwise.

When I step into the woods now where I played as a child – and I try to visit every day even if it's only to drink a cup of tea among the trees – I wonder did they miss me when I was gone. Did they think I'd abandoned them? My beautiful oak tree with the twin boughs stretching around one another as if lost in an embrace – did it look for me? The trees have aged too. They're taller and thicker than when I was a girl.

I put my hand on their bark and feel the familiar coarseness. It's like greeting old friends. I cannot walk through the wood without placing my hands gently on their grizzled trunks or leaning my forehead against the moss that covers them.

I never exactly fell out of love with my homeplace but there came a time in life when I felt like I didn't fit in here anymore. My dreams were to become a journalist. Exactly how, I did not know. But the seed of an idea had been planted by a book I'd read. It was about a young girl who heard a voice in her sleep. Her name was Dakin and she was summoned by a mountain to leave her home and free the mountain that had been under a spell for hundreds of years.

My teacher at Drung National School, a two-room school house right across the stone wall from Maggie's house, asked me to write a review of this book, *The Farthest-Away Mountain*. I must have been ten or eleven years old when I read this tale of trolls and gargoyles and was entranced by the bravery of Dakin who, like me, lived in a small but beautiful place where she was in love with nature. But when the mountain called, she listened. I wrote my review and my teacher said that it was like something a journalist might write. What was this? I wondered. A job where you could write and tell stories – I had to discover more. How to make it happen would be trickier.

When I went to Carndonagh Community School in the mid-1980s. I felt like I had been swallowed whole. At the time, it was the biggest second-level school in the country. Our proximity to the border meant the Troubles – the violent sectarian conflict that claimed thousands of lives in Northern Ireland – were never too far away. That same proximity and the geography of Inishowen had the effect of cutting us off from the rest of Donegal and indeed the rest of the Republic of Ireland. Unemployment, early school leaving and a lack of opportunities were rife.

Into this mix came Fruit of the Loom, a giant textile operation with outlets in the towns of Buncrana and Malin. It became a huge draw for young people promised good wages. Many left school early. By the time I did my Leaving Cert, the eleven classes which had started in first year had whittled down to just four.

Donegal in the 1980s didn't feel like a place for making dreams come true and it could be a harsh place for a person who wanted to do something with her life that fell outside the norm. I wanted to become a journalist, to travel the world, to meet people and tell their stories. I don't know how many times people, including some teachers, told me to do something more sensible. Despite this, I wasn't discouraged even though I wasn't sure how it might be possible when getting through the school day felt like an exercise in survival of the fittest. You kept your head down as a younger member of the school population. Sticking your head above the parapet would have risked drawing attention to yourself and that was not where you wanted to be. For the first three years of school at least, I did my best to be invisible.

By the time the Leaving Cert rolled around, you were in safer territory. If you were one of the few students taking the final exam, you were a lot more comfortable in your own skin.

My English class was the best thing about my entire school experience. My teacher, Mr Gallagher, was not typical. Indeed, he went out of his way to set up our class-room in a hemicycle shape to encourage us to talk. This would be a forum for discussion of the prescribed texts. It was a space where I thrived. Looking back, it's the place I first found my voice.

I remember returning to Carn School and knocking on Mr Gallagher's door after I got my Leaving Cert results to tell him I'd be going to university to study English. I said my thanks, but I don't think I was fully able to articulate the influence he had had in my life or the gift those classes had been. He had offered us a space to talk about poetry, about writing and how it made you feel. That space had only ever existed in my head. He had flicked a switch and I was buzzing with possibility as a result. He had opened up worlds in that room. It was a safe space to talk about words and what they might mean, what they could mean. Coming through that classroom door was like crossing a threshold to another world.

For a kid who loved having her head stuck in books, those classes were like a treasure chest. It occurred to me that perhaps there was a world out there where you could immerse yourself in writing and in telling stories.

When I look back to my last summer at home before moving away, I remember it as a time of magic. My friends and I would be moving on, but for that summer we were celebrating life. We went out at the weekends. I had a part-time job in the local hotel so I had some disposable income. My college place was guaranteed. Life was good.

There were whole days and evenings when my friends and I would sit on the beach at Shroove, a small cove where the Atlantic rolls in near the village of Greencastle, and talk and dream and try to think of what our futures might look like. We'd sit there until the evening light faded and the sand grew cold and our teeth chattered. We could talk for hours about what these new lives might look like. We were so full of hope.

In the autumn of 1991, I took up my place at college. I opted for a degree in English and French at Maynooth University. I still went home almost every weekend of first year. The buses from Dublin were packed with students from Donegal, like me, making their once-weekly trip home. I hated the return journey on a Sunday. The bus we took did a tour of Inishowen before finally crossing the border into Derry and heading for Dublin.

As the bus journeyed through the village of Clonmany and then into Buncrana, I would look at the people enjoying late-afternoon walks on Lisfannon Beach with their kids and their dogs and think how simple life would be just to be home. It was a fleeting thought and I never indulged it. My purpose was set – college life was heady and I threw myself into the thick of it until I got stuck.

I didn't see it coming or recognise the warning signs. When I look back, it seemed to descend like a dense fog and for the life of me I couldn't see how I'd find a way out. It started with fatigue; I was so tired all the time. I could sleep all day and sometimes found I did. It was third year, my final year, and while it was now time to get serious and knuckle down to do some work, I couldn't do something as simple as get myself out of bed. It never occurred to me to go home for a while. I think if I'd taken that option, I might never have left again. Going home would have felt like failure too. Had I not chosen this path for myself?

I was unhappy and anxious. Life looked uncertain. My periods stopped. I was retreating fully into girlhood, not wanting to step forward into the adult world. Always outgoing, now I didn't care about anything except sleeping. I was twenty years old and I was tired and exhausted with life. I was also so sad all the time, crying profusely, about what exactly I didn't know. I began to believe that if I didn't wake up it would be a relief because it was only when I was asleep that I didn't feel tortured, anxious and sad.

I know that friends found it hard to understand what I was going through. I had always been so sociable and here I was running a mile from anything to do with meeting others. I pushed some of them away; others didn't care to know. I eventually told my family how I was feeling. I was diagnosed with depression.

Diagnosis sounds like the wrong way to describe something that has a stranglehold on every fibre of your being. But that's what it was. I began seeing a counsellor and every Monday of that academic year, I travelled into Dublin city by bus, taking another bus to Tallaght where the counsellor was based. I had never been in a situation where I'd been for counselling before, but I knew something had to change. What was happening to me? Who was I becoming?

Over the course of those months, I began to look at my life and make sense of where I was. It was a slow, gradual process of being able to come back to myself. I see it clearly now; I was afraid. I was afraid of becoming the person I always wanted to be. In my head, my dreams felt as huge as stepping off the edge of a cliff and hoping to sprout wings. I was also homesick — not in the sense of missing home, but in the sense of missing some fundamental part of me that seemed like it could only be happy in Donegal.

I wanted to go back to a time when I woke to the smell of the sea and watched the light changing by the minute on Lough Foyle. I wanted to taste the nectar from the honeysuckle as I walked the fields. The dreams I had of being a journalist seemed at odds with all this until the wise woman counsellor reminded me that Donegal is not just a place on a map, it's in me. She told me that it was in the inflections of my accent as I spoke. The skies and sunsets and lick of salt in the winds of home were held deep in my soul. And so, uprooted as I was, I carried this like a pearl deep inside me, worrying it between my fingers if I ever felt unsure of where and who I was in the world.

I will forever be grateful to this woman for reminding me that the places we come from leave their marks on our hearts and our souls. Even when we are far from them, we hold the memory of them like water in the bowl of our being. Over time, something began to shift. It wasn't overnight. The heavy, leaden feeling I'd been carrying was lightening. The trouble was easing. I was no longer lethargic. Enthusiasm for life was bubbling up again slowly, like a spring rising deep from the bowels of the earth. I felt like I was finally coming out of the fog of depression that had set in and left me floundering.

My recovery started slowly but gradually in the way that your body reacts almost automatically when you hear certain music. My body and mind were starting to tune into the music of the world again. My dreams started to take shape again and I suppose I began to feel hopeful. Hope is a big word when you're depressed. It's a word you don't indulge in. It's too big. But that's exactly what it was.

By the end of the academic year, I was lucky to pass my exams and graduate. My experience of college had been tainted by the last year where I struggled deeply, but the experience informed how I saw the world. It gave me a greater understanding of how fragile our mental health can be. I never took mine for granted again. With good professional help, I realised that the gifts of my childhood, the freedom I'd experienced, my love of nature, my sense of deep rootedness and love of place and family could all be ballast against other storms in life. These could guide me back to myself when I lacked courage in situations. I could call on them when I felt unsure.

Do the cormorants feel unsure or full of self-doubt as they flap wildly over the breaking waves? These brave little birds have always been my favourites. I had spent many days in childhood watching them sitting on top of huge rolling waves looking like they would be pounded by the wall of water coming towards them. What always amazed me was how they knew just how to position themselves so that as the wave began its roll, they seemed to bob along the top before it broke. They know this is their place and sitting on top of the ocean as the waves come one after the other is what their life is about. I had to find the courage to do that too. I had to acknowledge that I was afraid of what the future held and get on with it anyway. And I did.

Home gave me that courage. I was ready to take the next steps. I was still unsteady on my feet but I wanted to try. Remembering where I came from, my family, my place in the world, gave me wings. And indeed I soared in this new world. I found my way.

But in the course of a lifetime you can get lost more than once. Finding your way back doesn't get any easier just because you're older, even if you have more tools at your disposal to navigate the route.

As you age, the world can become hostile to sad bereft women. There's a reason mad women were always locked in attics in literature. It's so their screams don't annoy people. But if we don't scream, we don't heal. If we don't talk and tell people about the things that hurt us, then we're going to get stuck. Everyone gets stuff to deal with in life. The longer I live, the more I see that this is true. Being comfortable with our own painful pasts and journeys is part of coming home to ourselves. And this is why I want to tell you my story about how I found my way home again; how embracing the wildness in myself and all around me helped me map the way.

CHAPTER 2

We choose us

If you'd known what lay in store,

would you still choose me?

Would you still say yes?

How could it be otherwise, my love?

This road, this path we are on, is leading us home,

And home is always you.

One of the first things I loved about my husband, Richard, was his voice. Easy and mellifluous, when he speaks, you want to listen. I distinctly remember our first conversation. I was twenty-three and he was twenty-nine. We talked about our homeplaces. We met to have a cup of coffee to discuss my doing some work for the business section of the *Sunday Tribune,* of which he was editor. Our coffee meeting was in a bar not far from the Baggot Street offices of the *Tribune* and we sat down to chat. It was before the coffee culture took over and meeting for a coffee in a bar or lounge was pretty commonplace.

Curiosity about one another's accents led us to discuss where we were from. He spoke about his home, outside Carrickmacross in County Monaghan, where he'd grown up with four brothers and two sisters. I told him of mine in Donegal and we instantly bonded over a shared sense of strong rural identity, the importance of family in our lives and a fierce love of nature and the natural world.

While these things shaped us differently, they provided us with a strikingly similar value system. When Richard talked about nature and roaming wild as a child across the fields, making bows and arrows with his brothers, I could picture myself there among the woods and the drumlins, the backroads and the riverbanks. I fell in love with him. I loved every thing about him. We would talk about everything: poetry, history, theology and of course journalism. We haven't stopped talking since.

We're chalk and cheese in so many ways. He's quiet and thoughtful, while my habit is often to launch myself into something feet first. He's shy in a crowd, preferring to stay quiet, while I'll flit like a social butterfly in a field of buttercups. But what was to become obvious later in our lives was that both of us needed to retreat to nature to recharge ourselves. When the world overwhelmed us, we needed to disappear, to go back to our homes to connect again with nature and with family and the places where we had deep roots.

What part did our dreams have in our early conversations? It seems that sometimes the dots join up only after the event. But it's clear to me now that we were destined to find a way to make a different life away from the city.

On our wedding day, Richard gave me a leather-bound notebook with an inscription to make it a record of our lives together. It was the most perfect gift and typical of Richard. I decided that it would become a travel journal. No matter where we went, it would come with us and I would record our trips and travels and who we met along the way.

Together we explored the world, throwing caution to the wind. We foolishly never saved a penny. We were lucky that we bought our home on the northside of Dublin city before the property boom made it impossible for young couples like us. But every spare penny we had, we spent on heading off to faraway places, on trips which we planned meticulously for months, looking at maps and drawing up itineraries.

We travelled Mexico by bus, stopping in the ancient

city of Oaxaca and even Acapulco in the days before the drug lords took it over. We spent two summers in Montana – one wasn't enough because we fell in love with Big Sky country. We learned to fly-fish, took hikes deep into bear country and rafted down the Middle Fork of the Flathead river.

On another trip we spent a month in New Zealand, travelling the country by camper van. I remember driving the road out of Queenstown and staying at a campsite in Glenorchy, which seemed like the edge of the world. At night when I looked up into the sky, I felt truly far from home. The southern skies were completely alien. In that moment near Gillespies Beach, where a nearby grave-yard was full of headstones with Irish names, I had such a longing for home and the stars I'd see over Lough Foyle that it felt like a physical pain. But with Richard by my side, these feelings which came over me every once in a while soon left.

Alaska had been on our radar for many years and we planned a big trip there that would see us raft out of the town of McCarthy and spend almost a week on the Chitina river, camping by night and paddling by day. For days on the river, we didn't see another person, apart from our few fellow paddlers and guides. One night just as dusk fell, we witnessed an ice fall from a high peak. This place felt like the wilderness at the edge of the wilderness.

Our last big trip was in 2007 when we decided to walk the Inca Trail. We flew to Lima and then travelled on to Cusco to acclimatise before hitting the trail. When we arrived in the ancient city of Machu Picchu after hiking and camping out in the Andes, we found a quiet spot, took off our hiking boots and rested. Just the two of us, away from everyone else, we found our own little corner of this magical place that was just for us. One of my favourite photos is of our hiking boots sitting side by side overlooking the most stunning vista at Machu Picchu. It sums us up.

For our last few days in Peru, we headed north to the city of Puerto Maldonado and took a riverboat down the Madre de Dios river into the heart of the Amazon jungle. It could not have been a more perfect end to the most amazing trip so I was surprised when one evening Richard wondered out loud if this was all there was. We'd spent the best part of ten years travelling the world and he was keen for us to 'mix it up a bit'. I hadn't a clue what he was talking about. Of course we'd had conversations about having children. But even when some of my friends were getting pregnant, I never felt like I was missing out or that there was some clock ticking.

Richard caught me off guard when he said he felt ready for a family. Was I? I couldn't say. Being perfectly honest, at the time, I could have spent the rest of my life travelling the world. I'd already started gathering some clippings of travel pieces of the next place I wanted to go – the Indian Himalayas were next on my list. I have yet to go.

But the conversation did stir something up. Motherhood was something I'd taken for granted. I definitely saw it as something I'd want for myself. I knew that I wanted to create a family with Richard, but for the most part I already felt we were a family – just the two of us.

I wasn't one of these women who is born knowing she wants to be a mother. I didn't look at other people's children and feel a longing course through my veins. Mostly I felt lucky that I wasn't tied down by small people with their own wants and needs. This was at odds with the idea in my head that we'd have three children. I knew I wasn't getting any younger but I was unmoved in the places where I thought I should be moved by thoughts of children.

And then I turned thirty-three and something strange began to happen. I, who had never previously felt a maternal stirring in my life, began to dream I was pregnant. In the dreams, I was so heavily pregnant I could barely move. I felt so happy in these dreams and content. The feeling was of being replete. I felt full of this dream baby and I longed for him or her. When I woke up, my hand would go automatically to my flat and definitely not pregnant belly. In that liminal space of being not fully asleep and not fully awake either, I felt bereft.

This didn't happen just once or twice. It kept happening, and each time I would be inconsolable upon waking, crying copious tears that wet my pillow. It wasn't rational and it was very confusing, but it also opened up a possibility that I'd never really honestly admitted to myself before. I wanted to be a mother and I was ready to embrace it.

During all of our years in Dublin, working hard in our jobs as journalists, Richard and I made the trip north to Donegal or to Monaghan as often as we could. We'd pack the car with our hiking boots and raincoats, driving late through the night to make it to Donegal so we could wake up there on a Saturday morning.

I'd look out for the early signs of the River Foyle, the first marker that I was nearly home. Once the lights of Derry city came into view, I could exhale. The river that flows out of Derry and into Donegal would guide us home.

Saturdays were always spent trying to get lost in Inishowen, exploring somewhere new, whatever the weather. Our conversations always came back to one thing. Could we ever make a life here that would work? How could we make it our everyday and not just the weekend? Was it a pipe dream?

There's a poem by Cathal McCabe called 'In Donegal' where the poet imagines a life he has never lived in an Irish-speaking part of the county. I didn't want my life to be haunted by what could have been. I wanted this place that held my heart to be part of my everyday.

Before we'd leave to head back to Dublin on a Sunday evening, Richard and I would walk the beach at Kinnagoe Bay. This majestic beach knows all our secrets for we've spoken them here a million times. We planned as we walked. We'd think about our futures. We'd look out to sea and wonder how this place, the Inishowen Peninsula surrounded by water, could ever be our home.

It didn't seem sensible, this dream of ours. We had good jobs and a lovely home in Phibsborough, in Dublin. We had each other. By any stretch of the imagination, we were blessed. But it wouldn't let go, this pull. Sometimes in the evenings when I'd get in from work, I'd find myself standing in the backyard of our terrace home, where I wouldn't have been able to swing a cat, and wondering what the light would be like at that very moment as the sun set on Kinnagoe Bay.

I'd picture the hill road over the glen before you descend to the beach. I'd picture the sand gleaming as the sun went down, turning the entire beach a shade of fiery red. And then I'd get on with the rest of my evening, reminding myself that this was a good life.

For New Year's Eve of 2008, I'd planned a surprise for Richard's birthday. I'd booked us a trip to Rome, where his brother Noel and his wife, Eimear, would be joining us for a surprise dinner in a little restaurant called Papa Giovanni's. It's gone now but it was nestled up a tiny, cobbled backstreet in the city, and when you looked in the window, it seemed to glow.

We'd been coming to Rome often, staying in a small guesthouse not far from the Colosseum. It was a city we'd grown to know well and to love. One spring a few years earlier, we'd even run the Rome marathon, which left from the Colosseum, took us around the Vatican and through all the tourist sites of the city.

Richard was turning forty and we planned to mark it in style in one of our favourite places in the world. A trip to Rome was never complete without a walk through the ancient forum, marvelling at the ruins and trying to picture what it must have looked like at the height of the empire. There are only a couple of intact buildings remaining – the senate building, or Curia Julia, is one; the temple of Romulus is another. This rounded temple is my favourite. I longed to find the large key to fit in the copper lock and turn it, stepping inside its ancient walls, but it was never open to visitors.

On this particular trip, we found ourselves visiting a church we had never been in before. Mass was taking place in the basilica dedicated to the saints Damian and Cosmas, and we took a seat near the back. The entire back wall of the church was glass. Deep in the bowels of the building below us, visible through the glass, excavation was going on. The walls of the building below were round. We were looking into the temple of Romulus.

On our way out, we met a priest from Kerala who we persuaded to show us the inside of the temple. We descended another set of stairs where the priest turned a key in a lock. Suddenly we found ourselves looking at the giant door we'd only ever seen from the other side. The smell of damp and age was all around us but it was otherworldly to find ourselves here in the temple named after the founder of Rome.

As we prepared to leave, the priest asked us if we would like a blessing. We knelt and he blessed us in this place that was holy to us and wished us happiness in our lives. We didn't know it yet but I was expecting our first child. I tell our eldest son the story of his coming to us and how in that moment in Rome I must have felt the first stirrings of him. As I stood in awe in the darkness of the temple, my son was taking shape in the darkness within me. In my heart his story is inextricably linked with this place.

Our first baby arrived in a rush in the early hours of a beautiful September morning at Dublin's Rotunda Hospital. He was born boxing the air. I was focusing so hard on deep breathing and on the pain that was ripping through me that I had my eyes shut tight. 'Open your eyes, Kathy,' Richard said to me. And there he was. The most perfect creature I had ever seen. Two intense dark eyes looking straight at me. I was split open with pure love. My own son.

We called him Dallan. St Dallan was a saint and a scholar who was killed while visiting monks at Inishkeel Island near Portnoo in Donegal. I loved the sound of this name, the strong D at the start, the lyrical double l in the middle. Richard loved it too.

We took our son home from the Rotunda to our house on Sarsfield Street, not much more than a stone's throw away from the hospital, and loved him more than we ever dreamed was possible. Of course having a baby changes everything and the birth of ours caused us to look again at our lives and how we were living them.

After my maternity leave ended, I went back to work in RTÉ – at the time I was working as a journalist in the newsroom. I don't know if I wasn't ready or maybe I'd never have been ready to go back. Older mothers told me to give it six months, to see if I'd settle. I wasn't convinced that time was going to make a real difference. The sands of time were shifting on this life. The days were already numbered and I knew it in a place inside myself that I wasn't yet ready to acknowledge.

From his earliest days, we started to bring Dallan to Donegal and to Monaghan. While we loved our house in Dublin and the feeling of closing the door on the city and being in our safe nest, it seemed to shrink after our son arrived. It wasn't just about the amount of stuff a baby brings into your life. When we'd go and spend a weekend in Donegal with Dallan, the world seemed to have diminished when we'd get back to Dublin.

For a decade, Richard and I had been talking about what a life elsewhere might look like, but honestly I was scared. I was afraid of what leaving my job might mean and what we would do to make a living. But the longer I lived in Dublin, now with a child, the more I realised this was not the life I wanted anymore.

As a parent, I hated the conversations about where people were sending their child to school. Important conversations but I found them stultifying. Pre-boom, people were already moving to socially engineer their address to get their kids to certain schools. The city as a melting pot was to my mind becoming more prescribed. There was a path and you were on it. Get with the programme.

There was also a path within RTÉ. Keep moving forward, keep climbing, keep going. I hate this idea of prescription. Every cell in my body rejects it. I remember reading about a rare interview the writer Joan Didion gave in the late 1970s where she said: 'I'm not interested in the middle road – maybe because everyone's on it.'

I was never interested in the middle road either. I always preferred to take the road less travelled. I have never wanted to be part of the pack. Even though I had worked very hard as a journalist to get to a certain level, an uneasiness had set in, a restlessness. Was this all there was? We had a good solid existence. Was there something wrong with me for wanting more? What more could you want?

In the winter of 2011, I found out I was pregnant again. A scan confirmed it was another boy. We knew he would be Oirghiall, named after the ancient kingdom which took in parts of Monaghan, Armagh and Louth. We also knew that we would be leaving Dublin sooner rather than later.

Oirghiall was born that summer. He was two days overdue and arrived after a night that I thought would never end, when I walked the corridors of the Rotunda, begging for the pains of labour to cease. I had wondered if my heart had room to love another child like I loved Dallan. Could I love another little person like I loved our first? I need not have worried. The space in my heart expanded to make plenty room for Oirghiall, our summer baby. We knew that our boys – although always proud of their Dublin roots – would be raised somewhere else, somewhere a world away.

And so, on a bleak January day, we left the house we'd become a family in. The removal truck had gone up the road the day before. We'd packed up our lives into boxes and sent them north with a prayer. Be good to us, I prayed, as we lifted the last box on board the truck.

Our two little boys – Dallan was three years old and Oirghiall, then only five months old – were oblivious. I'd spent the previous week making videos of the rooms, saying goodbye to everything. This house had been our oasis in the city. When we finished a stressful day at work, once we closed the red door at the front of the house, all felt like it would be OK.

We'd created a beautiful home; not in the sense of fancy furnishings or things – neither my husband nor I would win any interior-decorating contests – but it felt like us. Our favourite books lined the shelves. The walls were dotted with things we'd picked up on our travels. It smelled like us.

For over a decade it had supported us, its walls had listened to our stories. It was the place we'd become a family in, and while I know that a house is just bricks and mortar, this one had once belonged to Richard's great-aunt Lily, and his mother had played in it as a child. It felt like we had roots here too.

I said goodbye to the soft wood of the bannisters that I had touched every day. I thanked the spirits of this good home for looking after us. I reached out the window of our bedroom and touched the cherry tree whose blossoms we looked forward to every spring. If I could have transplanted this whole edifice a hundred and eighty miles up the road, I would have done it in a heartbeat. My heart sang in this old Victorian red-brick. But it couldn't hold us or our dreams anymore and we were leaving.

I remember holding our youngest child as we took photographs outside the front door. Looking at these pictures now, we look so much younger, so different. Our boys have changed too – they have grown from babyhood to gangly and wiry boys – but Richard and I have changed as well. Not just in the way the years will do that to you. It's something else. An innocence, almost. When I look at those photographs, I see so much hope in our eyes. A family on the crest of setting out on a new life. There's a sense of the calm before the storm that we couldn't see coming.

I cried as we left Dublin behind. They were tears of goodbye, of letting go, of relinquishing something beautiful. I muttered another quiet prayer, hoping we were doing the right thing. A bit late for all that now, given that there was no turning back. But I sent my words out into the world anyway.

It rained the whole way up the road, not just rain but sleet and sheets of it. The wind buffeted the car and I thought to myself, 'What the hell have we done?' Richard drove and I must have dozed off for a while, the tears having sapped my energy. Before I knew it, we were crossing the Craigavon Bridge and into Derry city.

It was a Sunday so traffic was quiet as we headed out of the city for the hills of Inishowen. Being so close now, we were buoyed up. My great-aunt Maggie's house would be our new home. Home, I realised. What will that feel like?

In the months before we left, as we gave serious consideration to our move, weighing it up and then deciding the time was now, strange things happened. When we would think something couldn't be done, something would happen to make it fall into place. Little serendipitous signs kept appearing. It felt like the world was making a map for us to follow. We just had to be brave enough to see it through. They weren't big things, crumbs perhaps but they seemed to open enough of a chink for us to see the way through the fog of doubts that still existed in our heads.

I don't know if I could do it again. We were both walking away from our jobs. There was the potential for work but remote working wasn't really a thing like it is now. We knew that technology was changing enough to allow us to be able to work from Donegal. In any case, the plan was for me to be at home with the kids for a while until we got settled. Richard had the guarantee of one newspaper column a week. We would sell our house in Dublin and be mortgage free. But we weren't sure how it would all pan out. Could we earn enough money? The house we were moving into was too small for a growing family in the long term. It had two bedrooms, one not much more than a box room, and a scullery kitchen. So many questions and yet I kept coming back to a quote I heard: 'Jump and the net will appear.' We did the equivalent of leaping off a cliff and hoping for the best.

Was it rejection to say I want a completely different life? Was it rejection to know in your heart that you want to wake up to the smell of the sea, to be shaken from your slumber by a flood on the river raging past? Was it rejection to want the flight of the heron on his way to his evening nest to be the last thing you see before the darkness comes of an evening?

Was it rejection to want for your heart the comfort of the oaks and the birches, the light hitting their silvery barks on a winter's morning, making them glow?

Was it rejection to want for your children a sense of space, for them to grow supple and strong as the oaks they'd play in and for them to know the names of all the plants and the trees in the woods?

If it was, then I rejected the life I had so far lived. I no longer wanted any of it. I didn't want the job and the trappings of establishment that had come with it. I didn't want the city life for me or my family. I craved something different and yet I had no clue what shape it might take.

Because we live in a world where people are so quick

to jump on the bandwagon, to criticise your choices if you so much as dare to ask a question, there will be those who are annoyed by the very idea of rejection. I know this because some people I knew took our leaving our old lives personally. There were some who couldn't fathom why we would entertain changing our lives so much. It seemed to cause them discomfort, as if we were casting aspersions on their choices.

But this wasn't about anyone else's choices. Our longing for a different life, specifically one in Donegal, was about understanding that the life choices we'd made up until that point no longer fitted us and our family.

It was a good life and a good quality of life. Were we mad or stupid to want more? But what if the good isn't fulfilling you anymore? What if you know in the deepest part of yourself that if you don't at least try you will spend the rest of your life regretting it? Maybe we could settle and think, 'This is good enough.' But what if a little voice in the back of your head reminds you of a different place and a different way to be that resonates with the wildness in you, the lone wolf in you. If this voice keeps growing louder and in fact starts to howl, then you listen and you follow. That's all I could do.

In life, there's always the road you didn't take, the path you never travelled. Would our lives, had we stayed, have looked that much different? I imagine they'd be full, busy lives. But something would always have been missing. I wanted to smell the woods on a summer's evening after a shower of rain. I wanted to step out of the house and walk barefoot to the trees that lined the riverbank and see if the sycamore leaves had burst their buds on a spring morning. I wanted to search the woods for signs of the owl and the fox. These simple things, so familiar yet so intoxicating, I wanted them in my everyday, in my family's everyday. If I'd never had them, I might never have longed for them, but that would be a different story. This is no apologia for my choices. They're simply mine and that's all. Not better or worse than yours. Just mine.

Life isn't about following the rules all the time. There are so many of them: should, must, better had. What about the listening to a different beat, the internal drumming of the heart that longs for things the head can't fathom? The heart remembers too. It remembers the wild places. It remembers the feeling of discovering a wooded area carpeted white with snowdrops. It remembers how to be full with very little. There are other roads in life to take if we listen for the deep voice inside that wants us to be happy. Sometimes to go to that place you have to rip up the old rules and start again. And so we did.

CHAPTER 3

A river runs through it

Deep swirling pools of darkness,
Shallow places to stand ankle-deep.
Ceaseless river music – the soundtrack to our days.
You have been the constant,
yet ever-changing presence in our lives,
reminding us that there is only moving forward,
no going back.

If you ever come this way, you can easily find us. Ours is the first house in the townland of Ballyargus, Redcastle in Inishowen. To get here, you follow the course of the River Foyle on its journey to the Atlantic Ocean as it leaves Derry city. Crossing the border into Donegal, you keep the Foyle on your right-hand side and head in the direction of Greencastle, where eventually you run out of road and the ocean stretches out vastly ahead of you.

Our house is up a short gravelly lane on the banks of the Drung river. It's a modest little place, a 1950s-style bungalow. The front door has two big windows on either side of it. Sometimes when I look at it from the bottom of the lane, I think it looks like it's smiling. It's a simple abode, but the setting is what makes it remarkable. Tall trees – mainly sycamores – line the riverbank and there's a small wood directly behind our house, accessed by a set of rough-hewn stone steps. It feels like our house is nestled into the edge of a giant green kingdom that towers above and behind it. There's another set of stone steps down to the river. I don't know how many years ago these steps were put in, but it's certain that my ancestors built them for easy access to the river.

I like to descend these steps to the river often and look up the dark river valley that stretches up to the hills behind us and think of my ancestors perched in this very same spot. I like to think of Maggie and her sister Annie, my paternal grandmother, coming here as girls and young women to share their secrets. They're long gone now but I remember them laughing together conspiratorially when I was a child.

When we came to Donegal we weren't trying to

replicate our own country childhoods for our children by leaving Dublin. That would be impossible; the world has changed. When I think of how we roamed the countryside, my sisters and I calling into neighbours' houses and spending time with them, that's unthinkable today. For one thing, my children are much busier with extracurricular activities than I ever was, nor do they know the inside of many neighbours' houses in the way I did as a child. That's no longer really part of country life in the way that it was when I was young.

But we did want our children to experience a childhood that would be informed by nature. We wanted for them a childhood spent outdoors, where they could roam safely in the woods, build dens and forts and climb trees.

We wanted things for us too: more time to spend in nature as well, wild camping trips, walks in the woods as night fell and swimming in the sea as part of our routine. I wanted to learn to surf. Richard wanted to buy a kayak. I had an idea to keep hens and ducks and maybe even a goat. My family had always kept goats. Granny Carey in Greencastle had two and Jim had several. For a short while, my parents kept a pet goat, Twiggy, until she tangled herself up in a ditch. I wanted a dog, but in our early days in Donegal we decided we'd wait until the boys were a bit older and could take on some of the responsibility that comes with keeping a dog.

We realised that the townland of Ballyargus was populated with a few families with the surname Curran. To differentiate us from other families, we decided to give our home a name. The one we settled on was 'Missoula' after a town in Montana we fell in love with.

We used to have a state map of Montana on the wall of our kitchen in Dublin where we highlighted all the roads we had driven in the USA's 'Big Sky' country. Missoula was like a gateway town for exploring the beautiful natural landscape of Montana. Surrounded on all sides by huge mountains, the town was first inhabited by Native Americans primarily from the Salish tribe. Its name roughly translates as 'river of surprise or ambush'. Three rivers run through the town and it was the setting for the 1976 fly-fishing novel by Norman Maclean, *A River Runs Through It*. The novella, which later became a movie starring Brad Pitt, tells the story of two boys growing up in Montana with a love of fly-fishing.

The river that flows past our little house starts its life at the top of Drung Hill, pouring over a secret forty-foot waterfall on its way to Lough Foyle. It is our very own river running through our lives. In the woods at the back of our house, there are at least twenty-five oak trees, numerous birch and alder as well as sycamores. There are lots of hazel trees full of nuts, bilberry bushes growing close to the ground and holly trees that give us sprigs of holly with berries aplenty at Christmastime. This was my Narnia as a child. At the edge of the woods, the bank falls away and drops steeply down to the river gorge below. From this vantage point, you can see how the river valley has been gouged out. Some large trees have been toppled by the force of the water passing through. This beautiful, deeply spiritual place speaks of our own ancient Celtic past and is home to the fox and badger – they roam all over this place – as well as countless birds, bats, squirrels and owls.

One night shortly after we moved, I went to the woods just as dusk fell. As my eyes adjusted, I stood and looked down into the river valley below, listening to its rushing sound. All of a sudden, I was aware of something quite large with heavy feet running towards me at full tilt. It was a badger. I didn't move but he stopped mid-flight and reared up on his hind legs, sniffing the air. His acute sense of smell as he neared me made him realise he wasn't alone and as quickly as he'd been bounding towards me, he took off again and made for the big setts at the back of the woods, which is bordered by a wide-sweeping field.

The name Missoula seemed to fit our wild little place. Having visited Montana, we've always felt that Donegal is Ireland's version of 'Big Sky' country. Maybe it's a big name for a small place but now it trips off the tongues of our boys, who've never been to Montana. This place has always been Missoula to them. When we come back home after being away for a few days or longer, they look out the car window and announce, 'There's Missoula', as we get closer. That makes me very happy.

It also makes me happy that our boys will have deep roots here. My father grew up in this place that was his own mother's homeplace. My great-grandparents' homestead still stands. The two-room cottage that Jim lived in until his death still sits behind our house, hidden behind a tall hedge. Maggie's home is ours now.

These two people were two of the most influential people in my life, next to my parents. Maggie and Jim were essentially my grandparents and they had a big hand in raising my sisters and me. In his historical novel *Trinity*, the US author Leon Uris talks about the 'Big Smyths'. When one of my father's cousins was doing a family tree, he maintained that the Smyths in the book were named after our family. I've yet to read the book but from what I know and remember, the Smyths were amazingly resourceful people. They had to be resourceful to make a life here work. On the periphery of the country, farmland was poor. They kept a few animals; some cattle and goats. I remember the birth of goats belonging to Jim during my childhood, and coming to see them in the darkened shed where they were with their mother. I distinctly recall the softness of their noses, the helplessness of their bleats.

In an age of make, do and mend, there was nothing Jim couldn't turn his hand to. From cutting his own turf to growing his own vegetables fertilised by seaweed, Jim was in every way self-sufficient. For years before she retired Maggie ran a café across the border in Derry city. Every Friday, she'd take a trip to the city on the bus and ask me to write down the name of a book I'd like.

In my neatest handwriting, I'd print out the title and she'd take it to the now-closed Bookworm bookshop on the city's Shipquay Street and bring home my prize. From the *Narnia Chronicles* and *What Katy Did* to almost everything Enid Blyton wrote and Roald Dahl's entire collection of books for children, over time Maggie bought me a library and I'll be eternally grateful to her for the gift of books in my life.

My primary school was built literally across the wall from Maggie's house. It's no longer a school, but the wall that I hopped over for my lunch every day of primary school still stands separating our house from our neighbour's.

When Jim died in 1990, his house was closed up. The shed where he meticulously stored his tools and where I was seldom allowed to enter as a child is still intact. The smell when you walk in the door hasn't changed, a dry woody smell, mixed with oil to keep tools working. Maggie passed away on the second last day of the year in 2001. I miss them both every single day.

I don't know if I believe in ghosts, but I know that this place is imbued with their spirits. Things haven't changed that much in this little homestead since they left. I know how happy it would make them to see us here, bringing up our children in this place. I wish they had met my boys and seen the next generation tearing through the woods. I like to think that some part of their energy remains, keeping an eye on Dallan and Oirghiall as they laugh and run in this place that's been all of our homes.

When I imagined the life we'd have in Donegal, being outdoors more was a big part of that. But we also had to try and make a living. In the early days of our move, I was busy trying to get the boys settled while Richard worked out his notice with the *Sunday Business Post*, where he'd been deputy editor.

Our house was too small to fit a home office inside so one of our first tasks was to build a small cabin in the back garden to function as an office. When we talk about remote working now, it seems like there's a template or at least people have found a way of making it work. When Richard and I left Dublin, it hadn't been tried and tested. Trying to work for national media in Donegal. Did this sound like madness?

Both of us had spent many years working as journalists for a number of national outlets, including the *Irish Independent* and RTÉ. We'd both been on the staff of both organisations for many years but we were out on our own now, without the security of a staff job. It felt unstable to say the least.

What quickly emerged on our arrival in Donegal was that I needed to get driving. You can very easily feel marooned in Donegal without a car. There is a local transport service, but doing the shopping with two small children and trying to get to out-of-town supermarkets is not really an option without wheels of your own. I'd taken driving lessons in Dublin but living close to the city centre and with good public transport, I'd never really driven. If we were going away for the weekend, Richard did the driving.

For the first while, when Richard was working out his three months' notice in Dublin, I relied on my mum and sister Anne-Marie to ferry me to wherever I needed to go. After passing my driving test on the second attempt, I bought a second-hand Ford Focus, which meant I could be independent again.

Our early days in Donegal felt like a holiday, like this new life wasn't quite real. It felt as though we were playing a part in someone else's life and would soon return to our old lives again. Looking back, it was just part of settling in, of finding how to be again. Strangely I found this process much more difficult than Richard did. He didn't come with baggage. When you're from a small place, you're always someone's daughter. I'd returned home but I felt like a different person. I felt awkward, like I was wearing clothes that didn't fit me anymore.

Coming back to a place where you've grown up has its challenges. People like to think they know all about you. I had lived in a city for a long time by this stage and had grown used to my anonymity. Here everyone knew me and I wasn't sure if this was a good thing or not. It would take a while for the clothes to fit again. I knew that, but it still felt strange.

You can't simply slot back in where you left off. The world has moved on. The bonds of childhood friendships have loosened. You need to pick up the threads of them again and pull.

Yet I was hopeful for all of it, not just for myself, but for Richard and the boys. I wanted us all to thrive, for each of us to find new pathways to grow and develop and find things we loved individually and as a family.

I was, however, also full of doubts about how we would make this work. Could we make it work financially?

We were in the lucky position of not having to find a house – Maggie's house would be ours. But it would need work, at the very least a modern extension with a kitchen and another bedroom.

We'd made the decision to sell our house in Dublin,

which we'd bought in late 2000, just after we got married. It was now 2012 and the country was in the depths of a recession. House prices had collapsed in value. If we had moved six years earlier, we probably could have sold our home at twice what we paid for it. But that had all changed. At least it was still worth enough to clear the mortgage. The other option was to hold on to the house and become reluctant landlords. We didn't want to be landlords, especially not on a property that was 170 miles away.

There was another thing that played in our minds. If we had tried to keep hold of the house, it might have felt like a tether to an old life, a safety net if things didn't work out. We had made the decision to leave so selling the house was part of that. Like Cortés when he arrived in the new world, we wanted to burn the boats. There was no going back.

I am conscious that this is a time of deep struggle for so many to find a stable roof over their heads and that for others having a place to move to in the country is the stuff of dreams. It was indeed a gift that allowed us to change our lives. However, it didn't change the precarious nature of our situation. We had left our permanent, pensionable jobs behind. I had no regular source of income. The only guaranteed income we had was Richard's once-a-week column. It wasn't going to be enough to make a living. Could we put bread on the table?

Our guaranteed income moving to Donegal was less than one third what it had been in Dublin. The rest was going to have to be dug out somewhere month-by-month. We knew we could live on a lot less in the country, but would it be enough? It was far from clear.

The 'how do we make this work?' question was one we kept coming back to and it scared us. What if we were making a terrible mistake? It wasn't going to be just on our heads. It would be on our children's too. We were scared of failing, but we were also scared that if we didn't try we would regret it for the rest of our days.

The one major development that made our move possible was broadband. When we arrived, we discovered we had access to 3MBs of broadband. This was enough for us to work from home, but not a lot else. For the first six years, we couldn't both be online at the same time. Then fibre broadband came along and it was transformative.

Even if we felt like we were on the wing of the plane at times, work was possible from a remote location. We knew that this was the key to unlocking the possibilities. A decade earlier, we couldn't have upped sticks. From day one, the gods of technology had smiled on us. If we'd lived even a half a mile off the main road, we would have had less than 1MB of broadband, and our move would have been an impossibility.

As rural broadband is rolled out to more and more remote locations and the pandemic has shown us that we don't need to be stuck to a desk in an office, more people may make the decision to leave urban spaces and move to the country. But a decade ago it was rare. I remember some of the reactions when we told people we were going. Many were confused. They couldn't compute this decision of ours. At one point, I heard myself referred to as the woman who committed career hari-kari.

And sometimes it did feel like that. It did feel to me like I'd taken the career I'd painstakingly built and pulled the plug on it. But the world of work I had inhabited, with long shifts, didn't fit with the idea of motherhood I had or with the kind of mother I wanted to be. Together, we had made the decision that I would be at home for the early years of our boys' childhood. We'd had a wonderful childminder for Dallan in Dublin, but after he was born, I never felt like I was thriving in work. I felt like I was missing out on his days when I'd walk out the door and take the bus into RTÉ. On so many occasions as I'd walk out the door, I'd hear his laughter coming from the kitchen. I was content he was in safe and kind hands, but I felt so sad to be walking away from all that would happen in his day, from these small moments I would never get back.

It was only after Oirghiall started playschool that I began dipping my toes back into paid work again. I'd started my career as a freelance journalist working for *The Irish Times* and *Ireland on Sunday*, which later became *The Irish Mail on Sunday*. In 1998, I was named Young Journalist of the Year for my coverage of a gripping murder trial, in which a young woman was on trial for killing her husband. In its own way, the award opened up new possibilities and, shortly after, I joined the *Irish Independent* as a full-time freelance, soon landing a staff job at the paper. I spent some of the best years of my working life at the newspaper's Middle Abbey Street offices in Dublin. In the spring of 2006, I joined the staff of RTÉ where I worked in the newsroom covering beats as different as RTÉ radio's *News at One*, the *Six One* television news and the foreign desk.

Over time in Donegal, I started to freelance again. It was a bit like coming full circle, this time with the benefit of experience and contacts. I was able to pitch ideas to the various editors of the different sections within the *Irish Independent* and this gave me an income stream.

At the same time, Richard re-joined *Independent Newspapers*, now *Mediahuis*, as a columnist. He also took over from George Lee on the Saturday morning Radio One programme *The Business*. Soon after our move, Richard made a TV documentary about the future of rural Ireland. While it felt like we were living the real-life version of this, it also felt like very early days for us. But there was no going back; we had sold our house. There was no plan B.

All of us have our ideas about what a rural life looks like. If you come to a place in summer for a couple of weeks, you might go back to your regular life with the idea that the sun always shines and the locals are always surfing on the beach. Life isn't like that, and moving to Donegal wasn't us hoping for some version of *The Good Life*, where we'd turn our backs on modern society, start keeping hens and grow our own food. I haven't a clue how to be self-sufficient.

When I was growing up, this is actually how my grandmother lived her life. Her green fingers meant she could grow anything and everything. Her chickens laid fresh eggs every day; she baked bread on a daily basis and milk came from the two goats who adored her. In the space of a couple of generations, our lives bear little resemblance to that. But many of us have memories of real farm-to-fork before it became a trendy foodie term. It's easy to romanticise the countryside; there's a whole movement, 'cottagecore', that does this, but it's not real. Rose-tinted glasses won't help you make a living and at the end of the day, we've still got bills to pay and children to rear.

Swapping a life in Dublin for a life here in Donegal means that while I'm still at my desk these days during working hours, when I step outside I'm immediately in another world. In our lives we tend to delineate our work and our leisure. It's not always a good thing but my work and downtime tend to overlap due to the nature of my work as a journalist, which sometimes involves writing about my life.

There's a different rhythm to life; things just don't move as fast as they do in the city. When I first came back to Donegal, my internal clock hadn't reset to these rhythms and I'd find myself getting frustrated in a shop queue while people seemed to take ages to stand and chat.

I couldn't understand why you couldn't just pop into the post office and complete a transaction in jig time. It took me a while to realise that it wasn't others who were out of sync, it was me. By its very nature, life in the city is faster. Transactions are perfunctory. You're rushing for the bus, to pick up the kids, get to work – life moves faster. That's not to say you don't have deadlines to make just because you live in a rural place. Of course you do. But you're not likely to get caught up in a traffic snarl-up if you don't leave the house before 8 am.

Over time, the internal clock slows down a little. The frustrations of standing behind someone while they pay for their carton of milk or newspaper, chatting all the while, fade because you've become that person who'll stand and chat as you make your purchases too.

Sometimes I think I have to work harder or smarter since I left Dublin. I left a job where there was an actual pay slip every two weeks. I was a PAYE worker with a real job description. Now the ground is shakier. I have to hustle. Life as a freelance journalist is about taking on jobs on a piecemeal basis. This is my bread and butter now and I have to rely a lot on my wits and ideas to keep abreast of things, send in ideas, get ideas commissioned and do the work.

Richard taped a comic strip from a newspaper to the noticeboard in our kitchen. It sums my life up in two frames. With the title 'How to be a freelancer', it shows two identical pictures of the same harassed-looking woman with a laptop open and a cup of coffee on her desk. In the first picture, she has her hands up to her head, her eyes popping, with the thought bubble 'I haven't got any work'. In the second, the same terrified-looking creature is saying, 'I've got too much work'.

If you're self-employed in the gig economy, you'll recognise the script. It's all or nothing, feast or famine. Sometimes I long for an actual 'real' job where I go to a 'real' office with 'real' colleagues and have water-cooler moments again.

A couple of years ago, I started teaching journalism at a local college in Derry. It's part-time, but for one day a week, I leave the house to work. I buy a takeaway coffee and it feels almost like a version of my old life.

Even though I can imagine a more comfortable working existence, now I wouldn't swap my somewhat ad-hoc routine. It has taken time for this to bed down and it wasn't an overnight switch. No two weeks are the same; it depends on what I've got going on work-wise. But what I have got better at is remembering to do nothing in the lean times. When I've got some downtime, I get out and remind myself why I left the city in the first place.

While nature is all around us no matter where we are, I had stopped observing it in the city. Winter in the city never felt quite as harsh as winter in the country. For one thing, streetlights mean you can still get out and about. If I step outside the back of my house in Donegal on a starless winter's night, it's like stepping into an abyss. The skies are pitch black, all the better for seeing the night sky. I hadn't realised how much I'd missed it. There was the plough again. I followed it, making a note of the North Star. There was the Milky Way. A million constellations were visible from our back garden. Back in Donegal, I started to notice the phases of the moon. I paid attention to its effects on the tide. On the nights when she was full, I'd walk to the shore to see her reflection on the water.

I remember those first winter mornings here in Donegal. We'd made our move in winter and while it seemed foolish perhaps not to wait till spring, I'm glad of it now. That particular first one was so harsh and the north wind blew so strong that I thought it would take the front door off. When the signs of spring gradually started to come, it was like witnessing a miracle.

From our earliest days here, I developed a habit of going outside as soon as I'd get up, pulling on a coat and heading for the woods with a cup of tea in my hand. I began taking my shoes off and sinking my feet into the dew. It always seems cold underfoot first thing in the morning as I walk across the grass to where the big sycamore trees grow on the riverbank.

It's become my habit to observe these sycamore trees every day. I love it when the first buds appear in early spring and then when the buds grow a little bigger, looking almost otherworldly. I'm always amazed that such a big leaf is folded up intricately inside. It's like nature's own version of origami.

My morning ritual brings me to the entrance to the woods and I climb the stone steps dug out by my ancestors many years ago. My favourite time is spring when the promise is held in every bud, and in every furled-up fern, which appear like shy children, heads folded into their necks before gaining the confidence of adulthood. I'm on early watch for my favourite wildflowers: the snowdrop and the bluebell. By May, the woods are a riot of bluebells and if you come in the evening after a sunny day, they seem to emit a bluey-purple hue, and the scent of so many of them together in one place is intoxicating. In the years since we've been here, they've spread.

Initially, they were in only a couple of spots, but now they're shooting up everywhere and I smile to myself as I imagine the feet of my boys carrying seeds that take root everywhere they've run. My sons: life-size pollinators.

Spring sees the birds in full throat trying to outdo one another. I make my way to the seat in the woods Richard made for me from wooden pallets, and sit down, overlooking the river valley below. The seat is painted a sky-blue colour. There's something incongruous about it when set in its surroundings but something very welcoming too. The river is ceaselessly making its way downstream and into the Foyle. One large oak rises up in front of me, its branches stretching upwards into the sky. Some of the branches look like the limbs of a dancer, gracefully reaching out in a dance of appreciation to the sun. Beside it is an oak with twin boughs entwined around one another. It's so beautiful here that I don't want there to be too many days in life where I don't start the day here. I think of all those days where the woods were strangers to me.

They are no longer strangers to any of us. For my children, this is the place that informs so much of their lives. They know all the names of the trees just by looking at their leaves. They know the rain is coming by the smell on the wind. As they have grown, they've welcomed summers by going barefoot, making their own bows and arrows, running like Daniel Day-Lewis in *Last of the*

Mohicans, one of their favourite films. They know every inch of this place, better than I do now. They have named the trees and each has his own favourite. They refer to them using their names – Cú Chulainn, Ferdia, Stag's Head, The Unknown – which trip off their tongues as they tell me about their adventures in the woods. They are the wild kids we wanted them to be. Their love of nature is fierce. When our youngest son was given the part of Tin Man in his drama school's production of *The Wizard of Oz*, he baulked at the part as it meant he'd have to cut down a tree for his role, even if it was only acting.

I, too, have fallen in love with nature in this place all over again. Mother Nature, one of my first teachers, has guided me back home again. I know all about the rhythms of the year; I don't mourn the coming of the winter as it has its own beauty, and I know the spring will always come again. Nature has taught me patience. Things cannot be rushed, but I learned that the hard way. And it took many years. Because for so long I was in a rush. I wanted things to happen on my terms according to my timetable. Perhaps this was the lesson I had to learn all along.

CHAPTER 4

The rosebush isn't growing

Know in your heart that everything will be OK.
On the days when you don't believe,
look back on these lines and say
something has brought you to this point.
It's like an inexorable force has taken you here to this place,
to this time in your life and it's saying:
'Live, smell the roses, run fast, laugh loud,
joke, play, believe, love and don't stop.'

There was a little rose bush that grew in the front garden of our home in Dublin. It was bountiful and magnificent and planted by Richard's great-aunt Lily. The smell of it was intoxicating and ancient. You couldn't walk past it without leaning over to breathe deeply of its luscious scent. It was coming with us to Donegal. With extreme care, Richard dug it up, its roots like some ancient wizened creature that was rescued from deep in a bog. One of the first things he did when we arrived at our new home was to find a sheltered spot in front of a hedge to replant the rosebush. We hoped it would be happy in its new home like we'd be happy in ours.

Spring came and went and there were no signs of life on the rose bush. It seemed to be retreating. Some of its branches blackened. There was no life here, it seemed. I started to worry about it. I felt like I was doing much the same thing. I'd planted myself somewhere new and nothing was happening. I felt like my own limbs were withering on the vine. Who was I now? The day my maternity leave from RTÉ ended, I wept. I was unmoored. The work that had tethered me, organised me, given me purpose, friendships and a sense of who I was had ended. What was I going to do with the rest of my life?

That day, the day I would have been due to go back to work, was like a turning point. While I'd been contentedly throwing myself into the all-consuming job of mothering two small boys, this seemed to signal a change of tempo, like it was alright not to be working up until that point. But now what? Where did I go from here?

With a full heart I had made the decision to leave a job and a position I'd worked hard to get. I knew I couldn't be the mother I wanted to be and continue in the way I was working. I was in the lucky position that this new life could and would allow me to be home while the children were small. Yes, I was fortunate that I could make this choice. But that doesn't mean it was easy. I've thought about this a lot in the intervening years and I realise looking back that so much of the suffering I put myself through was unnecessary. I did it to myself in the way that women tend to beat themselves up over every single thing they do.

Stepping away from work triggered an existential crisis I didn't see coming. The opportunities for a full-time job in a national media organisation were slim to zero in rural Donegal. What would I become? What would I do with myself?

Part of the problem as I see it is that we feel like we're failing if we say, 'I'm a stay-at-home mother.' I hear women say it all the time, they almost apologise for it. Invariably they use words like: 'I'm just at home at the minute.' I've seen women disappear and run from conversations rather than join in. They would rather leave a group than face telling people they're 'just' at home. As if the word 'just' does justice to all the things that they get done in a day. But society is not set up to celebrate this. You're not successful unless you are spinning several plates, having a glamorous career, having children with an extracurricular activities calendar that needs a spreadsheet to calibrate it, as well as making the PTA meetings. Welcome to the world of modern motherhood.

You're not really nailing it as a modern mother unless you're as busy as a hamster on a wheel. I am so sick of the conversations about the cult of busyness. Even after the pandemic, so many people, and women in particular, are wearing it as a badge of honour. So many women are left feeling less because they feel someone else's disapproval about her choices, even if they're not really her choices. In fact, she might not have much choice at all. I remember talking to a woman I met who told me she wouldn't have the confidence to go into the local pub because she feared how other women would look at her. This woman is a beautiful kind mother and yet she felt shame about how she was living her life without a job.

Society's expectations are that we must work to be useful. Your purpose in life must be higher than 'just' being a mother. And unfortunately we are our own worst enemies and I beat myself up more than anyone else about this.

My identity as a woman has always been so intertwined with what I did for a living that if you asked me who I was, I'd say journalist. The question 'who are you?' would result in the same answer. Mother, wife, sister, friend all came secondary to that. I am fiercely proud of being a journalist. It was the dream of my childhood and a job I've done with joy ever since I first walked into a newsroom as a shy twenty-one-year-old many years ago.

Arriving back in Donegal to live decades after I'd left, I wondered how I could reinvent myself. Strange thinking about reinventing yourself in a place where you are known but yet also unknown. The truth is I felt lost and I was afraid of what I'd become without the safety net of a job. I realised that the job had grounded me and given me what I'd needed for so long that being without it scared the life out of me. This was uncharted territory. The boundaries were unclear. It was like walking in the mountains with no clue of where you're going. But yet here I was and had I not sought out the mountains? Had I not craved the wilderness, the wild beauty and the open spaces?

Yet, this was something different. It felt like a wilderness in me that I couldn't navigate. I had no tools to find my way out of this expanse and I would be sorely tested before I found the map.

Many women I know have these feelings about work and identity. It's not peculiar to journalism, but in a career where you have to work so hard to prove yourself, it does become pretty easy to define yourself by what you do. I prided myself on doing the best job I could do. My career was rock solid. I have to ask myself honestly, if the edifice of myself was built on what I did, is it no wonder that it came crashing down like a house of cards? I needed to build some more solid foundations.

Much of my life had been spent chasing stories, following them up, writing them all down. I gobbled up stories and I was always hungry for more. I worked very hard, always pushing myself to do better. I prided myself on never getting beaten on a story or missing a deadline. It all sounds a bit macho even to my ears.

To some people, never knowing what your working day is going to look like would be terrifying. To others, the work of a news journalist sounds a lot like Sisyphus pushing the rock to the top of the hill only for it to roll down that very day. The work of pushing the rock to the top of the hill starts again the next day. Perhaps it could seem like that. But I loved the clean slate-start every day. I loved being sent out on a different news story every day and picking up the threads of that story and weaving them together to meet the day's deadline. I woke up looking forward to work every single day. I never knew who I might meet. I never knew what way the day would go. It was exciting and kept me on my toes.

Some stories left me worn out. Others buoyed me up. I remember covering the Special Olympics in Dublin and coming home to Richard every evening with a sense of awe at how much human beings can achieve. When I followed harrowing murder stories or grim court cases, I'd use the evening at home to regroup, talk it over with Richard and pick myself up again before the next day.

Some stories became more than stories and the people who I met along the way became firm friends. Many stories shaped how I viewed the world. During my years at the *Irish Independent*, I went back to college as a mature student to study law as I found myself being drawn to the criminal courts and murder trials. My speciality was to cover the duration of the case and to compile what we call in newspapers a 'backgrounder', which would run when the trial ended.

This would involve talking to the family members of the person who'd been killed and the gardaí involved in investigating the murder. Some of the details of those trials will stay with me always. Not necessarily the gory or grim details but little vignettes of love that shone through. Some details will stay with me always, like a mother visiting the body of her murdered son in the morgue to find his beautiful teeth chipped and broken or the killer who mercilessly stabbed a teenager to death but walked for hours carrying his pet dog to find a vet.

I have often thought that the work of a journalist is like having a ringside seat as history unfolds. We're writing the first draft of history and it is a responsibility I have always taken very seriously. I still do and while journalists in society can come in for a lot of criticism, the vast majority I have worked with over the years are deeply caring, conscientious human beings who want to do a good job and get things right.

I have never allowed myself to become cynical, even though I have at times become deeply suspicious of politicians. I don't buy the clichéd view of the journalist as a hardened cynical hack. For me, it was always about making a difference in the way that I could, by telling people's stories, by giving people a voice. I have never been interested in celebrity stories or in interviewing famous people, although I have come into the orbit of many over the course of my work. The theatre of real life, covering the courts, hearing people's stories, was my life's work and my passion.

Perhaps that's why when I found myself in a place that felt a million miles from the action of the newsroom, I started to ask myself, 'What have you done?' Of course I'd thought it through. I knew things were going to look different; I wanted them to look different. But that doesn't mean that this decision to turn over a new leaf was easy. It was complicated by my own circumstances, by the nature of the job I did and how much I thrived because of that, and perhaps because I'm a woman who beats herself up too much.

In my career, I had found my purpose. I needed to redefine that purpose, but I wasn't sure how I could do that. On reflection, I see that I wore what I did like a suit of clothes, perhaps like a suit of armour. It allowed me to show a certain version of myself to the world. It was a version I was proud of. When that is gone, what face are you showing the world? The real you is often too much for people. You can be afraid the real you is not enough. I've thought about this a lot over the years too.

Sometimes when a baby is born and they're not doing well and there's nothing medically wrong, the doctors put the name of 'failure to thrive' on their ailing condition. I was failing to thrive in our early years in Donegal. On paper it all looked fine and there was nothing you could say was causing me angst, but I was fretting and worrying about lots of things.

One of those things was how I'd be perceived by others in my profession for having, as one person called it, 'blown up' my career. I should have realised that other people's opinions and judgement were theirs to hold and not mine to carry. It's easy to say these things in hindsight, but when you are grappling with a big life change you're on unsteady ground already and things like people's opinions will rock you.

I can be kinder now with hindsight and say that any leave-taking requires a letting go. Old aspects of yourself have to be shed like a skin. But I was so unsure of myself that I was holding on to the old, clinging to the trusted version of myself as I once was.

The road to putting down roots is not always easy. While the stars seemed to align to help us navigate the way to leave our lives in Dublin, settling into this new life was not going to be plain sailing for me at all. The analogy that always comes to my mind is that of a small tree. Would you expect to uproot something that had grown in a garden far away and expect it to thrive somewhere new in strange soil overnight? You'd have to prepare the ground, replant it tenderly, water it and feed it, make sure it got adequate sunlight and give it time. A bit like our rosebush.

When it came to myself, I didn't prepare the ground. It was like I'd replanted myself and just expected myself to thrive. For the first few months – it was winter and cold and wet – Richard was working out notice. I was at home with two small boys and, when I look back, I now understand that I was grieving.

So much has been written about grief during the pandemic. I've spoken to experts about how it affects us. They told me about the emotional and physical effects. Leaving a life behind, a home and friends as well as a job – this is going to cause grief. How had I not foreseen that?

I started to worry almost to an obsessive degree about

Lily's rosebush. On my morning walk to the woods, I'd stop by it and touch its little blackened branches tenderly, wishing it to grow. When we needed to have an unsteady and dangerous tree cut down – something we did when there was no other alternative – I asked the tree surgeon and gardener for advice on our rose bush. He told us we hadn't planted it in a good spot, that it was too dark. It needed more light, he said.

This sounds a bit mad but I started to look at this rosebush and its progress as being tied to my own. I was like ET and Elliott and the little sunflower-like pot plant the alien had. If the rosebush would flourish, I told myself, so would I. And so, at my insistence, the rosebush was dug up again and put into a pot at the front of the house where it's warmer. We would try again and hope for the nourishment of the soil and the heat of the sun to bring it back to life.

It would take more than the heat of the sun for me to thrive. I wish now I'd been kinder to myself and more patient with my progress. I wish other people's opinions hadn't bothered me as much. Luckily, despite my fears that the rosebush and I were both in trouble, there was still some part of me that had a deep knowing that I was in the right place, at the right time, doing the right thing.

It wasn't a flourishing thing; it was a seed of a thought buried in the dark. It was like a little voice that said, 'You know all there is to know.' I didn't have a plan for how I would find my purpose or how I could make it align with my ideas of motherhood, but I knew it was out there waiting for me. This little voice that had already said 'no' to the open door that was laid out in front of me in terms of career also spoke of holding on.

What kind of woman was I now? Was I less than I had been? Why did I care so much what other people thought anyway? I had already decided to go my own way. I needed to have the courage of my convictions and keep going, one foot in front of the other.

This particular path I'm talking about is not about my relationship with my husband, my friends and family. It's probably the most fundamental relationship in my life; my relationship with myself. At this point in the early days in Donegal, it wasn't a healthy relationship. It was kind of passive-aggressive.

Recently a good friend told me a story about how her neighbours behaved in a particularly obnoxious way, leaving her reduced to tears. My friend is a strong woman and to hear her having this experience vexed me. I asked her, if the shoe was on the other foot and I was the one telling her this story as if it was my experience, what would she be saying to me? She responded that she'd be telling me the problem was theirs. She'd probably also tell them to take a running jump, she said.

It's very easy to be a good friend to others. It's much harder to be our own best friend. But this sometimes stranger in the mirror is the best friend you have. If you don't treat her with kindness and understanding, if you don't nurture her and pour love over her, she'll wilt. I wasn't very good at being kind to myself. There was always the harsh voice in my head that criticised my choices, who looked at other women who seemed to be managing so much better.

I was so busy trying to be the version of myself that I thought slotted into this life in Donegal that I forgot how to be myself. I was a little bit afraid of drawing attention to myself, of being too much for people, that I opted for a uniform of sorts. I had so many pairs of grey skinny jeans and grey oversized jumpers that they all blended into one another. I thought that if I could get the uniform right – on-top-of-it-all mum, too busy to be worrying about clothes – then maybe I'd look like I was fitting in. But I'm not a grey jumper and grey jeans kind of person. Who was I kidding? My wardrobe has always been a riot of colour. I adore dresses and flashes of exuberance. I wear hats for as many occasions in life as I can. I wear head dresses on special occasions. But it was as if I wanted to hide. I can see this now. I was hiding in plain sight.

Being me and giving full expression to my life was on hold. I was like a garden in winter. The parts of me that were playful and colourful had seized with the frost of doubt. The parts of myself that were confident, mainly because of what I did for a living, were so withered I doubted they'd ever sprout again. The parts that were kind and loving still functioned but only for others, not myself.

There's a poem by an unknown author that I love. It begins, 'She sat at the back and they said she was shy. She led from the front and they hated her pride.' The woman in the poem goes to the woods and tells the trees how she felt she was never enough, she was either too little or far too much. I have felt like that for much of my life and when I talk to friends it seems these feelings are universal. Even acknowledging it makes the feelings a little bit easier to carry.

I don't know anyone who knows what they're doing all the time. Some people just do a better job of making it look like they do, but ask some of the most successful people how they make it all work and they'll probably tell you that inside they're terrified. It's almost a relief when you ask them how they're feeling and they admit that most of the time they're just winging it.

While my daily trip to the woods was comforting, it was also reminding me that I was outside my comfort zone, that here was a new place I had to navigate. The woods became a metaphor for my own self and how I saw myself. They were as familiar as old friends, but time and distance had separated us and we were struggling in one another's company.

I got lost in the woods once before. Well, I didn't feel lost but I was indeed gone for long enough that a search party had been formed and was about to take to the fields to look for me.

My great-uncle Con had come home for the summer from Glasgow and we had made a plan to go and look at Drung waterfall.

This waterfall is like something from South America as it drops into the river canyon below. During periods of heavy rain, you can hear it from lower down the river valley. I have since seen it with just a trickle of water coming out during a particularly warm summer. I have also seen it when the weather has been so cold that the water has actually turned to ice as it falls. It is majestic and otherworldly and in a very secluded place. Surrounded by steep ravines on both sides of the river valley, it can be treacherous to get to, particularly after rain has left the ground unsteady.

Seeking it out is especially tricky from our side of the river. You have to go through the woods and either stand at the top of it and view it from just above or come alongside it.

That day I went to see it with Con, a day that went down in family history as the great missing-adventure, we had clung to trees and had navigated across the woods, trying not to fall down the bank. I can remember how awestruck I was as I watched the water plummet into the rock pool directly under the drop before flowing into the river and moving downstream. I must have been seven years old then and hadn't made it that far into the woods before.

After going to the waterfall, Con and I had climbed back up the bank and had walked through the big, broad field above the woods, ducking out onto the roads. We had walked several miles along backroads of the townland of Ballyargus before stopping in the village of Redcastle at McGowan's Bar. Con was great friends with Seamus, the owner, and so we'd gone inside where Con had had a glass of Guinness and I'd had a glass of lemonade. I'd proudly sat up at the counter – I distinctly remember my legs not being able to touch the rung of the stool – while we chatted away.

After a short while, we had walked the rest of the way back to Maggie's house where the searchers had met us on the lane. My great-aunt and uncle, my parents and a couple of neighbours had assembled. The last time we'd been seen was heading for the waterfall hours earlier. I hadn't been the least bit worried about being lost in any way. I'd had an unforgettable day with an uncle who was like my very own personal Roald Dahl, always with a twinkle in his eye and a story in his mouth. He had been crestfallen for having caused everyone worry. But for the rest of his life we were to talk about our beautiful day of discovery.

I have thought about our missing-adventure often over the course of my life and over time it has only increased in the glow that I feel, for my beautiful uncle and the gifts he gave me in life. I've often thought, too, about the girl I was. I wasn't afraid of much, not the dark, not being outdoors or far from home on my own. But in the early days and months in Donegal, there I was an adult woman with children of her own and I was afraid. I was afraid mainly of what I was becoming or, more importantly, not becoming.

One of the things I have learned about by uprooting my life is that change takes patience. People think you change things in a single swoop and that's it. But change comes slowly, often at a snail's pace, and if you are a person who has operated at breakneck speed for most of your life, meeting deadlines and beating them, learning patience is hard.

Over time, Lily's rosebush bloomed. It sat for a long while in a very large pot at the front of the house, receiving a good amount of sun and shelter. I kept an eye on it but eventually I stopped worrying about its fortunes as if they were somehow tied to mine. We were both growing independently of one another, I realised.

And then one day as I was getting into the car, I was stopped in my tracks by not one but several rose buds on the bush. I bent closer to inspect this small miracle and there it was, the ancient rose smell, tangible even though the buds had not yet unfolded. I understood that it was only time and patience that had made the difference. This hardy plant needed to put down new roots. It would also take time for me to bloom.

CHAPTER 5

Sorry, who are you?

She rises in the half light, bleary-eyed, hair sticking up.
All around it's as if something moved through the space
at speed; knocking, dropping, spilling everywhere.
She lifts the tiny screaming person into her arms
and holds this creature who doesn't want to be held.
Eyes closed, fists balled, the child shakes in rage at the world.
She feels rage at the world too.
For a heartbeat, there's a feeling of the two of them being
locked in a fight to the end.
His screams quell. He latches on. He settles.
She looks out the window at the trees with their leaves
starting to fall.
She imagines that deep in the wood it's so quiet you can hear
the leaves softly landing on the forest floor.

And she longs to find a little hole in those woods,

to crawl into it and sleep ...

There have been so many times over the course of the years that I've been a mother that I've imagined myself somewhere else or I've longed to be somewhere else. Does that make me a bad mother?

There have been times when the feeling was so strong that I wanted to bolt from the house and leave my own children to their mess or their scrapping? These two people who I love more than anyone else in the world have also caused me to want to flee my life and to question whether the life I was living was one of purpose.

I am older now. I wouldn't say I'm wiser but I think I've learned some things along the way that have helped calm me down when I feel overwhelmed with the job at hand.

I remember taking Dallan home from the hospital and Richard and I being strung out for lack of sleep and bursting with love for this little being in our lives. Friends of ours – parents of older children – came over to visit. The dad proceeded to tell us about the first time his son had a temperature and how awful and scary the whole thing was. Our baby was a few days old, lying blissfully in his Moses basket, and I thought I was going to have a panic attack from simply hearing this story. How would I cope if Dallan got a temperature? How would I get it to come down? Would I be able to manage such a dire-sounding thing? Then it hit me, all these mini traumas coming down the line that parenthood would bring. That story seemed to open a Pandora's box in my mind that I couldn't shut.

But I slowly realised that you manage these little tests. When the temperature comes along, you have a little bit more confidence and you just get on with it. I'm at a different stage of parenthood now; my eldest son is in the first throes of teenage-hood. What challenges will that bring? I'm listening to parents talking about staying up until their child comes home from the disco and I shudder because I'm not there yet. But some day, I know, I'll turn that corner too.

During those early years of being back in Donegal, which coincided with my boys being a baby and a toddler, I found many of the challenges overwhelming. My heart was telling me where I needed to be, which was at home, but my rational brain was screaming, 'What have you done?' These early years pushed me into fight-or-flight mode. They propelled me into a kind of perpetual state of crisis. They made me ask of myself, 'What is my purpose? Is it a mother?' If the answer was 'only' a mother, then that wasn't making me happy; it wasn't enough. Part of me feels thoroughly guilty writing these words down and also a little bit sad. My greatest joy isn't enough. What does that say about me?

Wanting more is synonymous with modern life and I don't think I'm alone. Mothers I talk to are grappling every day with this one. I often wonder how much of me has taken on projects, stuff, work, challenges to prove, 'Hey, I'm more than just a mother, you know. I can do all this other stuff as well.'

I see the cult of modern motherhood where you have to be back at work within weeks of having your baby, working hard to bring home income, staying fit and healthy, making time for friends, looking a million dollars and having an Insta-worthy body and smile as toxic. There's no other word for it and social media is making it worse. I know women who've had to leave social media for their own mental health. That's not to slam it. It can be a place to reach out to friends and to engage with people, but it's not providing real human connection for most of us. In fact, it can make us feel like we're failing on a whole other level.

It's not just social media. Motherhood has become a commodity with so many opportunities to sell you stuff. The way the world is set up pits women, and especially mothers, against one another. It's not enough that you have one baby. What's the delay? You need to have at least two more and not too far apart in age either.

You must have a certain kind of birth. Poor you, if you have a caesarean – although thankfully the narrative around this is changing. Not breast feeding? Feel the chill wind of disapproval that particular failure brings.

I knew when I had my first child that I wanted to do things my way. But as a first-time mother you have no clue what your way is and you can get trapped into feeling that someone else is managing so much better than you are. I know this because I did and I know so many other women who will say the exact same thing.

When Dallan was tiny, I took him to an ante-natal class to encourage breastfeeding. Our early days were not going so well and I wanted to see if I could find helpful hints and tips from an expert midwife. There were only a few mothers there; one of them I knew from a pregnancy yoga class we'd attended. She was on her third child. All I can remember is this big, open room and we were encouraged to crack on with it and get our babies to latch on. I removed my top and underwear and tried to get Dallan to latch. Of course he wouldn't and he cried. I admitted to the midwife that the night before, my husband had given him a bottle as I was almost beyond reason without sleep.

It was as if I'd stood up and slapped her. All the other mothers in the room looked towards me and my crying infant. I felt naked to the world – well, I was actually half naked – and I wanted the room to swallow me and my baby whole.

'Nipple confusion!' the midwife announced to the room. The other mothers were mortified for me. I felt ashamed that I had somehow let down the sisterhood by caving in and giving my son a bottle. I had fallen at one of the first hurdles. Failing my baby, so early too. I went home and cried and tried again to feed him. I'd like to say now – not to win mother of the year or anything but just to reassure new mums – that I wish I'd called out this bullshit. I breastfed my son for a year. He was not confused. We were just having a hard time getting started. I had the resources to pay for a kind lactation consultant to come to my house to help me work things out. Things went smoothly eventually, but that's the kind of shame I'm talking about that can really get under your skin and into your bloodstream.

A more confident me would have said something pithy and smart, but all I could feel in that moment of time was that I was failing my baby. I wish I could say this was the only time I felt a stinging sense of shame. It wasn't.

At a mother-and-baby massage class, the new mums were encouraged to tell their birth stories. We had only just arrived in the room when my son began to cry and fuss. He cried through other women's stories. The facilitator tut-tutted as if my baby were misbehaving; he was only a few months old. I felt embarrassed that these earth-mother types had little babies that oohed and aahed on the floor beside them while mine screamed like a banshee. I like to think that my eldest son, the most intuitive child, who was able to read the atmosphere in the room before he could talk, picked up on the air of total crap.

Why do so many women feel like they're failing at life? It isn't just in motherhood, although opening this door seems to leave you open to all sorts of criticism. It's not overt. Sometimes it's just a look and you recoil in shame.

I've read about practices in communities all over the world, where a woman who's had a child will have her mother, aunts and sisters come and stay while she recovers. Those weeks after the birth of her baby, she is not allowed to leave her bed. Nutritious food is cooked for her to restore herself. Here, women are often sent home feeling like they're already failing.

I was lucky that my mother practically moved in with us after Dallan came along. I wondered how it was possible that three adults could be so busy attending to the needs of one tiny person.

When I found myself back in Donegal with two small boys, I didn't know what kind of mother I was. I wasn't sure who I was anymore. I'd left behind friends and a circle of women I'd met in my work and pregnancies. The safety net of work had disappeared and it didn't seem enough that I would stay at home and be the main caregiver. I had things I wanted to do. Now I wonder, were these things I actually wanted to do or felt I should do? Were they one and the same?

In my mind, I wanted to be a 'free-range' mother. That's not shorthand for growing my own vegetables and puree-ing them for dinner. What I wanted was to tear up the rule books. When I was pregnant, I'd read copious parent-ing books. When one talked about letting your child cry and perhaps putting down a plastic cover in their cot in case they got sick while crying it out, I threw it away.

There were no books I could get my hands on which showed me how to be the mother I wanted to be. I was always one to read my way into things. It's how I figured out much of the world. I could find nothing that really got how I wanted to be. It's not like I had some grand plan; I just didn't identify with many versions of mother-hood I was seeing all around me. I've learned that some advice is good, but most things are on instinct. You figure it out as you go along and if you're lucky you'll have a supportive partner and a bunch of friends who are figur-ing it out as they go along too, so you don't feel so alone.

There was no template for this woman I wanted to be. I'd left a home and a job and all the trappings of a good life to go and raise my children in Donegal. Yes, I had family here and friends, but it was like ripping something apart, like disrupting something certain and sure. I knew I wanted the world for my boys, but what did I want for me? I wasn't sure how the plans I'd spent years nurturing fitted into this new life.

I felt like all the courage I'd mustered to leave my old life was spent and here I was. Nobody ever really talks about the mind-numbing hours of boredom spent at home when children are small. How can it be mind-numbing when you love them so much? Standing making pots of baby meals for freezing or putting on another wash of clothes is not the stuff of anyone's dreams. These tasks are stultifying.

I spent those early years of their lives cleaning noses and bums, picking up clutter from the floor, trying to make home-cooked meals for them – because we're told that if we're not making things from scratch we're failing too – fitting some fresh air and exercise into an already hectic day with so many small thankless tasks.

I had this conversation with a friend recently whose children are younger than mine. She wondered was it OK to wish that for one day she didn't have these mun-dane tasks to do, if for one day she got to do whatever she wanted. The very second the words were out of her mouth, she felt guilty.

I still feel guilty too. A lot of the time I feel like I'm failing. I'm too busy or I'm not busy enough. I'm not putting in enough time enriching my children's lives with activities or I'm too busy running in the car with them to extracurricular activities. I feel bad a lot of the time because I want things for me. I feel guilty when I bat them away when they want to play me a new tune on the guitar and I'm trying to get some work done. It never really goes away, this guilt that seems to be bred into us.

But even though the guilt is still there, I'm kinder to myself now. Years of self-flagellation have left their scars and I try not to beat myself up anymore. Some evenings when Richard would come in from having done a day's work, I'd literally run to the woods. In the fading light, I'd sit there and just look at the trees. It felt wonderful to have nobody needing anything from me just for a few minutes. I'd look up at the strong boughs reaching up to the sky as it darkened and I'd try to drink in their strength, to fortify me again to go into the house.

Being in this place altered something in me. It dialled down some of the noise in my noisy head. I was always glad to sit for a few moments and rest, watching the stillness. It's like a gift to watch trees in the quiet of dusk. They come more alive as the gloaming arrives. Your eyes start to play tricks on you and you imagine the great boughs are reaching for one another, reaching out to you. Sit long enough and a bat will swoop past your ear. I love this time of day.

After one particularly trying day, I had a sudden desire to lie down on the forest floor. I had an urgent need to feel the earth under my bare feet, to peel off my clothes and feel the cold earthiness against my skin.

There was nobody to see me here. Nobody to judge. I wanted to peel off the layers of my everyday, this suit of daily motherhood, and to feel like me again, but there were small children to be fed. I'd only sneaked a few minutes while I had their dinner on. And anyway what kind of madness would it be to strip off your clothes in the woods?

I'm older now and if I could go back in time, I'd whisper to that younger woman to take the time to lie in the woods naked if she felt like it. I'd tell her to stay a while longer and gather her sustenance from the earth and from the trees. I'd tell her that no feeling is stupid or pointless or not worth having. I'd tell her to be herself and give herself full permission to be whatever she wanted to be.

On another occasion, when the boys were a little older, I saw a seal stick its head up from beneath the waves to look at us as we walked the beach at Shroove. My children ran ahead shrieking in delight as the wind whipped up all around us. As I walked the length of the beach, the seal seemed to swim in the same direction, sticking its head up every now and then. It was almost as if it were following me.

I stood and watched it for a while and the seal watched me back. The wild waves didn't cause it a moment's thought. It was like it was dancing in the roiling sea. As the tide rolled out, I could see fronds of seaweed pulled back. It looked as if some mythical creature with long flowing hair was swimming just below the surface.

For a fleeting moment, I envied the seal its freedom. At that very instant, I would have slipped my earthly skin to join the seal in its watery kingdom, to feel my own hair swept back by the tide. All the while, the seal continued to watch me, masterfully negotiating the waves, making it look effortless even though these waves would have been enough to knock you off your feet.

'What's your secret to being so free?' I asked the seal. 'What's the secret to being so comfortable in your own skin, to looking so purposeful?' I wondered. If I had it, I'd bottle it, I thought, because I don't have an ounce of it. The seal's big liquid eyes watched me closely. I wondered if this seal had pups; if she were female, was she a good mother? For those moments I longed to be free of worries. I wanted to be unfettered in my day. I wanted to be buffeted by the waves and not care where I went because I felt careworn and so fed up of feeling not good enough or not enough, full stop.

I felt so tired of trying to be and do everything perfectly while making a mess of so many things. What if I just stopped trying so hard? What if I just stopped? Mother-hood had made me happier than I could have imagined, but it had also trapped me. Yet it was a trap of my own making. There's no mould. There's no right or wrong way. The perfect mother doesn't exist. I would have to figure out my way in the dark, by trying, failing sometimes and failing again.

There's a habit I developed then. It's one I still have. I don't know whether it's good or bad, but before I sleep I take an inventory of the things in my day that didn't go so well, particularly those things to do with the boys. I go over them and think of ways I could have handled things differently. Then I let them all go, the good and the bad. I go to my front door and I look out to the Foyle and I say, 'Goodnight world, see you tomorrow.'

So often, though, I wondered who I was. What was I? I still saw myself, heels on, notebook in hand, ready for the next story. I still longed for the social butterfly – who loved nothing more than a night's dancing – to emerge. Where had she gone? Then there was the serious woman, who overthought everything and whose solace was usu-ally to be found in the folds of a book. I was all these things and yet I was none of them now. Motherhood had torn up my finely written script and I was lost.

I was trying to figure myself out and possibly doing what I do really well – overthinking things. I had thought coming to Donegal would have the effect of turning off the tap of ambition, of wanting things for myself. Perhaps I believed motherhood would turn me into a much less needy person in terms of my own wants; that I would focus only on my children's needs. How could I have been so foolish? A woman's needs don't vanish because she becomes a mother. Yes, they change and often go to the bottom of the list, but they're still there waiting for a chance to be allowed to come out again. The old her is still there, perhaps buried a little bit, but she's there with all her longings and hopes and dreams of her own that have nothing to do with babies.

I must have thought that motherhood would see me casting off the longings of my old self like worn-out jumpers and becoming this new version of me that was bursting with joy and delight at being home all the time.

That's not the reality and that's not what it looked like or felt like. The reality was not what I thought it would be. I loved my children and my husband fiercely, but I also wanted to feel like the old me, fired up by stories and meeting people and deadlines.

Change has a habit of dialling up the emotions. Grief, pain, anger, desire, longing and love are all part of the furniture when you decide to change things. How I wish sometimes that I could go back in time and meet that younger woman on the beach and tell her to take it easier on herself.

I'd say to her, you've got to be your own best friend and you'd better be a bit kinder to yourself. You are beating her down with your constant berating and negativity. She needs you to cheer for her, to let her know she's doing OK, especially on the days when she feels she's failing most. You need to hold her hand and say it's OK, just like this wave coming in, it'll pass and there'll be another and that's OK too.

I didn't realise how hard I was on myself, how much pressure I was putting on myself to be more than I already was. I judged myself so harshly. They say comparison is the thief of joy – that's so true. Comparing yourself to someone else is like taking the cloth of your happiness and ripping a knife right through it.

When my children feel disappointment that they haven't managed to do what a friend has done or they covet something a friend has, I ask them if they'd compare oranges with stones. 'Why are you comparing yourself with another human?' I ask them. 'You are you and they are them and it's not a competition,' I tell them. I hear myself often saying to them: 'Stay in your own lane – that's not your race.' Perhaps my learning along the way has helped me to give them some useful tools to use. That's the job of parenting. I just wasn't very good at paying heed to the things I would have told a friend in need.

The mind of a woman can be dark and treacherous place.

How often do we pit ourselves against other women who we've no business comparing ourselves to? We do it all the time, whether it's about career, children or dress size. It's interminable and it's so damaging.

I carried my feelings of not being good enough across every beach in Inishowen as I would walk and sometimes run with my family. I would constantly scrutinise myself for not doing or being enough.

From before my youngest child could walk, I've been taking them to the beach. I do my best overthinking there. I'm drawn to the wildness, especially when there are big waves, and I could stare at the ocean and never get bored. Sometimes my family literally has to drag me away as I get lost in the watching.

The beach is also the place where I measure how far my children are moving away from me. When they were very small, we'd climb the dunes together, me helping Oirghiall, my youngest, up the steep dunes at the end of Culdaff beach. As they grew older, I'd let them run a little bit ahead of me, shouting if they went too near the waves. I've watched them bound over dunes, run through marram grass and explore countless coves. When I see them like this, at a distance, it's as if they've grown and I watch them become bigger boys with beautiful big hearts revelling in the outdoors. My heart breaks a little bit to see them in profile against the sun, moving inexorably further and further away from me.

Despite my fears and doubts that I was failing miserably, I didn't get it all wrong. There were many things I got right. My boys' love and total respect for nature is one of the things I'm most proud of. Their dad and I wanted them to love the outdoors. We could never in a million years have imagined just how much our sons would become immersed in the natural world. For them, trees are sacred beings; the death of a creature in the woods is solemn and they will not leave a dead bird in the garden without giving it a soft place to lie in death.

When we found a dead cormorant on the beach, we all stood over it, wondering at what had brought it to its death. We marvelled at the size of its strong webbed feet and its beautiful wings and beak. We didn't want to leave it lying exposed to the elements and it seemed brutal to fling it into the sea. My boys placed small stones all over its body and covered it over, wishing its spirit a safe passage to the place where cormorants go when they leave this world. They are more than I could ever had dreamed of and I love them with every fibre of my being.

Motherhood is hard. It's even hard for those on social media who make it look like it's one long picnic in the park. Perhaps it would be kinder just to remind ourselves that nobody has it sussed, that everyone you see is fighting a battle you know nothing about. I'm sure there were people who saw me walking the beach with my boys and thought, 'Oh, she has it sorted.' I put on a good face to the world. Make up on, head up. Inside, I was trying to hold on to who I was or who I thought I was.

The writer Maya Angelou talks about how most people do not grow up. She writes that we carry the accumulation of years in our bodies and on our faces, but generally our real selves, the children inside, are still innocent and shy as magnolias.

I believe this. I have felt like an impostor on countless occasions throughout the course of my life. A lot of the time, I feel like I'm kind of playing at adulthood and not really doing a good job at it and that someone will see through me. I think a lot of people feel like this. In my early days in Donegal, I sorely wanted to find that home inside myself, but inside myself wasn't a very welcoming place.

I wanted to fully belong and embrace this new life, but I didn't know how. I found myself back at home but feeling as far from my true home as I could be. I was not the girl who'd left this place, who dwelt among the people here. She was long gone. Without noticing it, I had journeyed a great distance and was uncomfortable now in my own skin, in my own surroundings. I was trying to wear clothes that no longer fit. I was awkward.

This was an uncomfortable truth for me. In all my life,

Inishowen had been where I felt connected and rooted. No matter how far from home I went, I felt my deep roots stir with longing for home. Now I found myself back at home, a mother and completely at a loss as to what I would do with my life. I got on with the everyday tasks of mothering. But while my children grew, I felt some sense of myself evaporating. They provided me with busyness of course and so many moments of joy, as well as questioning. And so I busied myself because to sit still was to feel too much. I wasn't ready to sit.

CHAPTER 6

Pieces of me

There's a dress I keep in a drawer. Inside a fabric bag.

Its peach-coloured fabric is of the finest silk,

like it was woven by butterflies.

Every so often I unpack it and imagine the small girl body

that would have inhabited it snugly, stocky little arms filling out

the short sleeves.

It's so fine and so perfect and exactly like I imagined she would be.

But she never came.

I can't bear to give her dress away

so I hold it sometimes and it feels like gossamer wings.

I will bring it with me for her in the next life.

She will swim towards me, arms outstretched, saying,

'I was always right here.'

I was falling apart. It was like looking into a cracked mirror and seeing pieces of myself. It felt like I was fragmenting and taking over less space in the world. The weight fell from my flesh and there seemed to be nothing I could do about it. I had no appetite and food tasted bland. It was as if my zest for life was suppressed. I stopped recognising this woman in front of me. Who was I? Peel away the trappings of your life – what you do, where you live – and you can get lost. Here I was, lost in a place I knew so well. Me who could find my way through the woods in the dark. Every inch of this place is carved into my soul and yet I didn't know where I was or what I was doing here.

Maybe we have to break apart to come back together again more whole? I remember a story from a children's yoga lesson, about the heart that at first glance seemed ugly and damaged. It repelled people at first until the heart explained that each tear and mend, each blemish and stitch was a mark of love. Love had caused the wounds and love stitched them back up again. When the children understood that the heart had been broken and then patched and mended, they couldn't see it as anything but beautiful anymore. We're all the same, the undamaged heart isn't nearly as beautiful.

If I was lost before, I couldn't have known just how far

from myself miscarriage would bring me. 'It's never nothing, it's always something and sometimes it's everything' is what I've heard a bereavement midwife say about it. For me, miscarriage became all-consuming.

Having another baby seemed like a great idea. Get on with it, we thought. We still had time. My thirties were ebbing away, but I'd had two healthy pregnancies and births that were like falling off a log. My obliviousness now causes me some embarrassment. How many women did I meet in my pregnancy journey who saw my swollen belly and longed for their own child? How many people crossed the road to avoid me because they were desperately trying to have their own baby? I was so proud of my baby bumps. The bigger they became, the happier I was. I don't think I'd ever be intentionally insensitive to someone else's feelings, but I have no doubt that I was so caught up in my happy baby bubbles that I was immune to the pain and suffering of others.

One thing I have learned is that when you roll the pregnancy dice or try to, you have no control over how it lands. It can go any way – all we can do is see what happens. And so, early in our move to Donegal, I got pregnant again. Another baby on the way. Three children. That's how I saw my life going. Did it seem selfish to long for one more child when you already have two healthy children? Maybe I was tempting fate by rolling that dice one more time?

I got pregnant in the spring of 2012. The line showed up weakly on the pregnancy test, not that I paid any heed. Hindsight is a wonderful thing. On a trip to Dublin, I started to bleed. I went into the Rotunda Hospital where I'd had my two boys. The first thing the nurse did was a pregnancy test. It showed up negative. I hadn't a clue what was going on. How could this be? It happens, they told me, and I sadly put myself on a bus back home. I hadn't been symptomatic. The pregnancy ended almost as soon as it started. My boys were in bed by the time I got home and I smelled their sleeping selves and soothed myself that it was early and that it wasn't meant to be.

I went into the woods and consoled myself in the company of my big oak tree with the twin boughs. I cried into the earth and named the baby that wasn't meant to be. Richard's heart was low too, but he told me not to worry. When I'm afraid, I look to him to reassure me. His calm is the perfect antidote to my habit of stressing easily. I had no reason to doubt him.

I remember calling into my mum and dad's house one particular day that spring. In the hallway, a baby house martin was sitting petrified by the door. Nests of these birds line the eaves of my parents' house and this little one had made its way inside and couldn't get out. As I gently picked it up, it was so frightened it didn't even struggle. The only sign of its fear was the pumping of its tiny fragile heart. It was so slight in my hands. I looked into its tiny face, its blue-black eyes looked into mine. It felt like the bird was asking me for its freedom. I opened the door, released it into the sky and it flew away. In that moment, it was as if I had released the spirit of the child I had lost into the open arms of the cloudless sky.

In late summer that year, I found myself pregnant again. This time it felt like a real pregnancy. All throwing up regularly and nausea, mixed with feelings of being ravenous with hunger. I was starting to show early. I bought a red blouse, wide and flowy but not screaming maternity, to celebrate this mini bump growing.

It was November when Richard and I drove to Letterkenny Hospital for the twelve-week scan. I'd had a scan at eight weeks and seen a little heart fluttering. All was well. We went into the scanning room. I remember a student being there on placement and being asked if I minded if he sat in for the scan. The lights were dimmed and my belly exposed as the cold liquid to make seeing the baby easier was squirted on. The sonograph moved easily across and around. I looked at the midwife's face. There was nothing. Only silence. I looked to my husband's face. Richard has a habit of stepping from one foot to the other when nervous. I noticed him doing that.

I'm spinning and silent and I can't quite take in what I'm being told. 'Go home, wait to bleed, come back' was the advice. I can still hear the midwife saying our baby looked perfect. Perfect. But this baby isn't moving. It's perfectly still. No sound, no movement. Just a deafening silence that fills the dark room. Some part of me ascended off the table and watched from above, hovering and looking at my prone self. I felt immense empathy for myself and my husband but I was separate somehow from what was going on beneath me. I even felt sorry for the student who now didn't know where to look.

On the way home, we stopped at a popular pull-in spot overlooking Lough Swilly and Richard rang my mum. I was numb. Everything was hyper-real. 'Remember this moment, Kathy,' a voice inside my head was saying. I looked out at the lough and the mountains of Inishowen and home in the distance. I wanted to head off into those mountains because going home would make all this more real. I would have to acknowledge it and sit with it and I just wanted to disappear into this expanse.

I was exhausted when I got home and that evening I pulled a mattress into the floor of my sons' room. I didn't want to be away from them and I fell asleep to the sound of their breathing.

The next day was Sunday and it was cold and stormy. Richard said he was going for a walk to the shore. Not long after he left, I felt like I was going to be sick. I had a contraction and rushed to the bathroom where I passed our tiny little baby. Dots where eyes would be, tiny little buds where fingers would grow, this little being fitted in the palm of my hand.

Richard walked back in to find me holding her or him – we'll never know. I was sitting on the bathroom floor holding this tiny piece of us, looking in awe at this little being. I will never forget Richard's face. He just stared before breaking down beside me on the floor.

By then, I was bleeding and it didn't feel normal. Blood was gushing out of me and wouldn't stop. I was haemorrhaging. It was not normal, but it happens and it was happening to me. We called my mum to mind the kids and made a dash for the hospital. The evening was dark and cold and it was lashing rain. I thought I'd never make it to Letterkenny. When I stood up to walk into the hospital, it was like a dam breaking inside me and I gushed blood. I don't remember getting to the treatment room where I was given injections to stop the bleeding. In a ward afterwards, I passed my baby's placenta, the size of a small dinner plate. I remember one of the nurses crying. I couldn't cry I was so scared. I'd lost my baby but I also felt like I had nearly lost my life, that I could have left my boys behind.

In our rush to the hospital, we had left our tiny baby with my mum. By the time I made it home again, the little fragment of a human had dissipated. We found an ornate box and buried the remains at the back of the garden.

Over the years, the little grave has become a place for ornaments; there's a fox and a badger and a small flagstone where I have scratched out our little person's name with a stone. Beside the grave we planted a winter apple tree given to us by my sister-in-law and brother-in-law who suffered their own heart-breaking baby losses. It's in full flower now, some of the pink petals have fallen onto the grave. Pio, we called him or her. A tiny name for a tiny being whom we loved and wanted to be with us in our home.

Christmas was just around the corner after the loss of Pio – our very first Christmas in Donegal – and I remember it as a hateful time. The world was getting ready to celebrate and I simply couldn't participate. I'd had to have surgery after the miscarriage. Despite all the bleeding, some fragments of our little one had remained in my womb and these had to be removed. I returned home wondering how I could continue to put one foot in front of the other.

As if the miscarriage wasn't bad enough, I was traumatised from what had happened. I knew it wasn't normal. For months, the sight of blood was triggering. My fight-or-flight mechanism had been pushed into overdrive and now even the slightest thing – the boys having a fall, a loud noise – could set me spinning. I felt shell-shocked.

I remember putting up the Christmas tree that year with the boys. I tried to be cheerful for their sakes. Dallan was excited for Santa and presents and all the wonderful things that the season of goodwill brings. Oirghiall followed his lead and was excited because his big brother was. I wondered how I'd ever look forward to a Christmas again. Would this time of year always be marred by loss? Was there a Christmas future somewhere that I wouldn't feel this pain? A friend gave me an ornament for our tree to mark our baby's life. It's just a simple white porcelain heart on a string. It goes on the tree along with the other special decorations that herald baby's first Christmas and decorations we've picked up on our travels that have significance in our lives.

I'm not proud of how I got through that Christmas. I drank too much. I wanted to numb the feelings I was having. I went through the motions of being excited to see the boys' Santa toys but all I could think of was how the baby I'd been carrying wouldn't be around to see a Christmas with us. The future stretched ahead and all I could see was an ocean of pain, of trying to come to terms with this. The New Year that I'd envisaged – preparing to welcome our new baby – felt like an expanse of emptiness.

The only way I could see to make sense of this was to try for another baby. I'd had two textbook pregnancies.

But life doesn't go according to plan and textbook twice doesn't mean that what comes after will go to plan.

When we found out we were expecting twins, it felt like a miracle.

Just before we were told there were two of them, I found two little acorns on a stalk in the woods at home. Beautiful, perfect and green, these little buds were bound together on one slender branch. I remembered what the Zen Buddhists say about the oak tree and the acorn: that it is the future oak tree itself that propels itself into being. It so much wants to be alive. When the doctor found two babies growing in my womb, I was brought back to the green ripeness of the acorns and hoped their wills to live would be strong like the oak, that they would grow tall like the trees in our woods.

On a visit to France to visit family members that summer, I felt like the luckiest woman in the world. The house where we were staying was right next door to the most exquisite holiday home that was shuttered. Its wealthy occupants would not come till later in the season. I peered through its gates, at the trees and lush beauty of the walled garden and thought of Oscar Wilde's story of *The Selfish Giant*. This was the garden of that story brought to life.

I thought of the children in that story who would visit the selfish giant and how he chased them all away. I put a protective hand over my belly and each evening after dinner I'd walk to a Marian statue on the side of the road not far from the beautiful garden. I'd pick some summer blooms and lay them at the feet of this statue of the Virgin Mary encased in glass. I prayed for protection for these two babies. Our scan pictures showed them nestled together, curled tightly, their two little hearts pumping away.

That summer, the evenings seemed to be never-ending. I would trail my fingers along the long grasses growing along the side of the road and feel my belly growing by the day. Twins. I was getting back what I had lost. In the car on that French trip I imagined summers in the future. We'd need to hire a bigger car for six of us. For a brief moment then we were a family of six, driving along country roads where fields of sunflowers stood like the sun's army on patrol. We played the music on the stereo loud, our two boys strapped into the back seat, happy to go along on whatever adventures we had planned. I felt so lucky, so happy, so full of complete love; our twins nestled inside me, curled around one another.

The night they left me was one of the longest of my life. I was back at home in Donegal and the sickness I had been feeling all those weeks had dissipated. I tried to swat away the worry that came creeping back into the edges of my mind like a dying fly. Earlier on that evening, I'd been at a meeting and someone brought out tea and scones after the work was done. Why wasn't I feeling nauseous? I wondered. I tasted a scone, mainly to see if it caused my stomach to somersault as was usually the case. Nothing. A silent dread crept over me. I wasn't really present for any more of the conversation at the meeting. I went home and had an early night

It took me a long time to fall asleep and in the middle of the night I woke to a feeling of a leave-taking. It couldn't be described as physical but some essence of being was leeching from me. The silence had a sound, a frequency just perceptible. It wasn't frightening, but I knew what it was. My twins were going. I'm not overly religious but I am deeply spiritual. Their spirits were leaving my body. In those moments, I wasn't afraid and I wasn't sad, although the sadness would come. I lay there and bore witness to a profound happening that looked like nothing at all was happening. While the birth of my sons was visceral and raw and life-affirming, this was quiet and beautiful and I remember every second of it as vividly as I remember the birth of my two boys.

It was no big drama or happening, just a deep understanding of their lives leaving me. The next day, I knew I wasn't pregnant anymore. The scan two days later confirmed it. Shocked, the obstetrician said it must have happened only in the last twenty-four hours. I told her I could pinpoint the very minutes.

I had to return to the hospital where I'd brought my two boys into the world. The doctor who I'd attended for my pregnancies with Dallan and Oirghiall had booked me in for an ERPC the day after the scan confirmed the twins were gone.

ERPC – evacuation of retained products of conception – an awful medical term for removing the remains of tiny lives. Richard and I returned to the hospital, a place of such joy for us, and waited for me to be called for my procedure. I had a strong sense of how I shouldn't be here. Why was I in a maternity hospital? I wouldn't be giving birth to anyone. The women sitting around me, their bellies swollen and full, were there for a different reason. I felt like death among them and I wanted to run away. I felt like an aberration in this place.

Panic started to set in as these feelings grew stronger, but then Richard said something that I will never forget. He told me that what I was going through, what we were going through, was as much a part of life as giving birth to a child. It wasn't abnormal. It was just life and every bit as much a part of the fabric of it as bringing a child into the world. I felt myself relax. I could do this.

I put on a hospital gown and was just about to go for anaesthesia when I made a quick visit to the bathroom. There seemed to be nobody around. I stood in front of a full-length mirror – why was there a full-length mirror in this bathroom? And I looked at myself. My belly was swollen under the gown. My twins lay still nestled beside one another and I had to let them go now. I have never felt more utterly alone. I wasn't even afraid anymore. It was worse than fear. It was desolation.

I didn't recognise the woman in the mirror. She was so far from the woman I wanted to see myself as. And yet she was me. I can be kinder now. What would I say to her standing there all alone? I would have more compassion for her. I'd say, 'Let it go now. It's not your fault.' I'd tell her that this will pass, that there's so much love in your life that you have to know you did nothing wrong. I'd tell her that not all lives are long, some little lives are lived fully and completely in your heart. But I didn't know any of that then. I just wanted it to be done.

I just looked at the red-eyed woman in the mirror and I told her to hold on. It was like some part of my brain removed from my physical self was looking on and telling the physical part not to be afraid. It doesn't sound rational, but then I wasn't rational.

We planted two white hydrangeas in the garden, right beside one another. They grow along the fence beside the river. They are nine years-old now, the same age as my twins. One bush is bigger than the other and stronger. I like to think the bigger one is sheltering the smaller one from the winds that blow up the river.

I suffered two more miscarriages. These happened earlier into the pregnancies, but even then, I had already pictured these tiny buds nestling down into the folds of my womb, their hearts beating strongly inside me – hearts that would beat for many years long after I was gone from this world. But instead of beating hearts there were regular visits to the early pregnancy unit, there was talk about fetal poles and gestation sacs and how it was too early to tell at this stage. More theatre, more surgery to remove what was left of the little lives that couldn't be.

By now, an almost madness had descended on me. I had become obsessive about becoming pregnant. I snarled and shouted and resented anyone who was pregnant. Social media became the most hateful place imaginable. I was rabid with a rage that I couldn't contain. At one point, which in its own way marked the end of the pregnancy road for me, I believed that once again I was pregnant. So sick of pregnancy tests, I trusted the bodily signs of pregnancy I was showing. I was feeling sick and nauseous and my lower back was sore – all the giveaway signs for me.

I booked an appointment at the hospital. I lay down for the scan, hopeful that all would be well. There was nothing there. I had to acknowledge to the doctor that I hadn't in fact done a test but the feelings were real. The doctor was very understanding. He explained that what I was experiencing was known in the medical world as a phantom pregnancy. Only recently have doctors begun to understand the psychological and physical issues that are at the root of what is known medically as *pseudocyesis*. Although the exact causes are still not known, doctors suspect that psychological factors may trick the body into 'thinking' that it's pregnant.

All I could think to myself was 'he thinks I'm stark raving bonkers' and I need to get out of here. I made my apologies and almost ran to the car. The doctor was being kind, but I couldn't bear to hear his sympathy or the explanations. This felt like I was losing the plot.

And so I read, I did yoga, I got counselling. I talked. I ran. I went to Lough Derg, where I stood in bare feet in the rain and made all kinds of deals with God. Somewhere along the way, Richard and I decided that we couldn't do this anymore. I was killing myself. My life had become obsessive to the point of awful. I had a life I needed to live, if not for me for my two boys. I had been going through the motions of motherhood, but I was a mess. I needed to honour my sadness, but I also needed to stop making myself sad. The third child I'd longed for wouldn't come. I'd already torn up the script on one life. Now life was teaching me that actually you control nothing. It was time to stop suffering and live. But how?

How do you get on with the day to day of living when you're so angry? I was raging against everyone and everything, including myself, mostly myself to be honest. If I had to see another baby announcement I knew I'd crack, so when Richard quietly told me someone close to us was pregnant, I picked up a plastic dinosaur and threw it so hard at the door frame that the foot fell off. That thing was bulletproof, but such was the force of my anger. I'd flail and rage and eventually run out of steam and collapse into a heap.

This pattern was repeated often. I'm not proud of how I behaved. Thankfully nobody got hurt in the throwing of things. My heart was the thing that was hurting.

But it wasn't just my heart. My whole sense of self hurt. I picked up a hazel in the woods one day to find its shell cracked open. I was like that: exposed and raw. Everything felt stripped away. Hurt gave way to shame. Now, I've read enough about shame in the intervening years to realise that this is one you've really got to run from. I know now that shame is as corrosive as acid to your sense of self. It burns you up, and I was burning.

I wasn't just heartbroken for myself. I was heartbroken for Richard and the boys too. I'd wanted another baby for them too. I wanted my boys to be the wonderful big brothers I knew they'd be and for Richard to be the amazing father he is to another little person of ours. Every corner of my mind that I turned over seemed to make the feelings heavier and sadder.

The miscarriages also made me feel shame. I was heart-broken at the loss of the future we'd planned. But I was also so ashamed of my body for letting these babies down. I asked my body to do a job, to carry these babies for me, and it didn't; it couldn't. When I peel back the layers of what was going on, I realise that I blamed myself. Blame and then shame. A lethal combination.

I felt like a walking wound, not a full human being. It was as if I were a walking womb and a faulty one at that. Everyone seemed to be getting pregnant.

I understand now that anger is mainly grief lashing out. Anger and grief – these two sit beside one another. They are like two sides of the one coin. Perhaps I put myself through the ringer of this pain by trying for another baby when we were already lucky enough to be parents to two beautiful boys? All I can say is the heart wants what it wants. Everyone's fertility journey is unique, often not straightforward at all. If anything, my own experiences opened my eyes wide to this and made me more deter-mined through my work to shine a light on miscarriage, a subject that is still not talked about enough, in my view.

I don't know what these experiences would have been like had I not had my children. I do know they would have been much worse. Perhaps it was a kind of madness to keep trying when we had two sons. In the thick of it all, all I could see was that the only way to be happy was to have another baby. I wasn't able to fully grasp how lucky I already was; how many blessings had been bestowed on my life.

It seemed like I was walking around in the world, but often I didn't feel fully present. I could be in a supermarket queue, going through the motions or making small talk, but in my head I wasn't really there. I was somewhere else. Lost.

There was one place I sometimes went that was a comfort during this time. I dreamed about it at first. It was a walled garden like the one in the children's book, *The Secret Garden*. There's a door concealed behind lush ivy which I can push apart to reveal an ancient lock. I turn a key in the keyhole. It makes a gravelly sound. When I push open the door, the air smells like honeysuckle and roses. It's in full bloom and there are wooden benches to sit on and admire the view. It's not a manicured garden. Vines grow up the walls. Wildflowers are protruding from cracks in the pavement that runs through the middle of the garden.

I'm only here for a short visit. In this garden, a baby rests in a tree. He is held by a sturdy bough and he's asleep. I know he's mine because when I pick him up he smells like my boys. I'd know that smell anywhere. I hold him to me and say his name, a name I never got to use, only in our family. He looks just like his brothers and when he opens his eyes he looks at me and blinks, staring up into my eyes. We spend some time in the garden, me pointing out the roses and the bluebells, showing him the daisies and the buttercups.

It started as a dream, but then I allowed myself to go here during the day. It was such a comforting place and I could visit at any time. In this place, when I have to return my baby back to the bough of the tree, I'm not sad. I can return again. And so I sing him to sleep, whispering him songs of love, of his brothers and his dad and how much he is loved. And then I lock the door with the big key and bury it outside the garden door where I will find it again.

Is this a form of torture or madness or love? Perhaps it's all three, but I did what I could to make my peace with what had happened, and my walled garden comforted me.

I try to be honest with myself about what kind of mother I was in those years to my sons, those years where I was caught up in a constant cycle of pregnancy and loss. I think for the most part I was a good-enough one. My boys were my one refuge. The smell of their hair, their little arms wrapped around my neck was my certainty in the world. I could get lost in their little worlds with them and these times were pockets of joy. There was a game we used to play in the evenings. We'd go for a walk on the shore and I'd tell them about the goblins who live in the woods and who come out at night. We'd have to make it back home before the sun dipped low, taking the light from the world. It started off as a way to get them back home in the evenings when they dilly-dallied too long, looking in rock pools or playing with sand, when we had to get dinner.

As time went on, they looked for me to tell them more about the goblins, what they looked like, had I ever seen them? The one certainty was we had to make it in our gate before the sun set. They loved this story, the urgency of it, and many evenings we ran across the last stretch of shore to get home. When I berate myself about how I was, I remember this story and all the stories I told them. I wasn't perfect, but I was their mum.

I do ask myself was I present enough for this important time in their childhoods. Could I have done better or more? I suppose I could. There's no such thing as the perfect mother or father. There's the good-enough one. Maybe at times I wasn't good enough but I also know I did the best I could at the time. The person I wasn't there for most was myself. I couldn't bear myself. I couldn't bear the sight of myself. Mostly I felt repulsed by my own body and I was so angry at how I felt it had let me down.

I understand now that this is a natural part of grieving. Anger is a stage. I wasn't so much angry at the world as angry at myself. How could I have let myself believe that it would work out? How could I have let these babies down?

There was no medical test that proved conclusive as to what was going on. Just one of those things. The thinking was that I had conceived and carried two healthy pregnancies and brought two children into the world, that this was just bad luck. Sometimes I still wonder was there a trick the doctors missed. Was there something in me or in Richard that would have led some doctor somewhere to tell us they'd found the 'smoking gun'? There was no answer and so in the absence of something concrete, I blamed myself.

I kept all my sons' baby clothes and my maternity clothes. I was so convinced I'd be needing them. I packed a bag with brand new baby clothes, among them little knitted shoes I'd bought in Italy. The woman behind the counter had looked at me, smiling knowingly, as if she believed I was in the early stages of pregnancy. I wasn't, but I believed I would be, and these shoes would one day slide over the feet of our newborn.

I sometimes imagined a girl. I saw her in pink in my dreams, although I could never have seen me overdoing the pink. Her hair is black like mine once was and she has big feet, just like me, feet that will mean she is teased about them when she's young. I see her face and her thoughtful eyes like her dad's. I see her growing, her head always in a book, dresses always torn on barbed wire. We are so alike, this imagined daughter and I.

As time went on, the madness of grief lessened. For the sake of our relationship, my husband and I had to stop this constant hoping, loss, hoping cycle. We had two boys who needed us. It was time to stop trying.

How do you know when the time to stop comes? I don't know. You just get so tired of trying and realise that you want to live again. It was an uneasy decision to come to. We had given it so much but it was taking so much from us. Enough, we said. It brought a peace of sorts, a sad kind of peace.

So I packed away the baby clothes and gave many of them away. My maternity clothes, I passed on. Some little pieces like a green tracksuit that Oirighiall wore when we first moved to Donegal and a hat Dallan had that covered his ears, I can't bear to part with so I've kept them. A polka-dot nappy bag with brand-new baby gros is in the attic and I am finally ready to unpack it. I'd bought the baby gros in the most beautiful boutique in a French town when I was pregnant with the twins. They were exquisite in a French sort of way, all brushed cotton and muted colours. I will wash those little pieces of clothing I bought and pass them on to a good home. It will be another part of the process of letting go because it is a process. It's not straightforward. It's a shedding of skins. Like peeling layers of yourself away, layers of hope maybe, and slowly handing them over.

Many years later, long after we have stopped trying for another baby, I receive a card in the post from the hospital doctor who brought my boys into the world and treated me through the loss of the twins. I have kept in touch with her over the years, letting her know that our family will never forget her. Her kindness and professionalism were a rock that I clung to when I thought I might sink. She writes to tell me she's retired. Even though I have long made my peace with the fact that there will never be a third child, this letter somehow marks the end of the road. I cry again. It still hurts and I know it always will. I just carry it better now.

Despite letting go of so many things, there is something I can't bear to part with. I still keep it in the bottom drawer of my bedside table and it's so exquisite that I will never let it go. It's a baby girl's dress. It's made of antique peach silk and it comes in its own silk patterned bag. There's a tiny collar and short sleeves that I always imagined podgy baby girl arms sticking out of. My sister-in-law Eimear bought it for me. Is it wrong that some nights when my heart is heavy, I take it out of the drawer and hold it up to my face to feel the softness of the silk against my skin?

It's the most perfect little dress. I can hold it now without crying, but I can't ever part with it. It belongs to my dream girl. When I hold it, it's like holding gossamer wings. I imagine her flying away in it.

In my dreams we are swimming underwater. I am hold-ing her hand and she is wearing her dress, looking into my eyes with hope and trust and love. In my dreams I see her and I say to her: 'Someday my love, but not yet.'

CHAPTER 7

Foxes, ghosts and stones

I am a fox now and I live in the woods at the back of our house.

I metamorphosed when you buried me but instead of

turning to earth, I grew hair and teeth and a tail.

Sometimes I come close enough to the house and

listen to you and I'm sad I'm not inside with my family.

But then I'm glad to be a fox.

You spotted me one day as I ran up the lawn, big, like a dog.

And you called everyone to see me because

you knew my soul.

The woods are mine and you sometimes see my tracks.

I leave my mark for you.

I know you look for me and it breaks my heart to hide.

But that is my nature.

I'm always here and I know that you know I am watching.

That is enough for me.

Foxes became like signs in nature. I searched for them, but they never arrived when I wanted them to. They came at a time of their choosing, catching my heart on the hop and at once soothing me and enrapturing me. I imagined that some part of my lost babies had metamorphosed into foxes and when I saw these wild creatures, it was as if they were saying their true nature was to be free and wild and I had to let them go.

So many of them live in the woods behind our home. One October morning, my head mired in thoughts of baby loss, I was getting the boys their breakfast before school. It was still warm and the back door lay open. I turned to see a young fox, not much more than a cub, delicately walking through the fallen leaves near the hedge. I called to the boys to watch this beautiful creature gently nosing the foliage. We stood stock still at the door. After a few minutes, he turned his head and it was as if it took his brain a few seconds to compute what he was seeing: three humans only a stone's throw away, staring at him. He took his leave and ran for the woods, all brushy tail and flashes of red, up the path before he disappeared back into the deep cover of the trees.

In my grief, I imagined that the soul of one of my lost babies had come to pay a visit. He was lonely for us and needed to check in. It soothed me in a strange way, and the grief that had lodged in my heart like a stone felt like it had eased somewhat.

On another occasion, close to dusk, I went to sit in the woods by myself. I sat and watched the darkness start to cover everything. Just as the light was leeching away, a fox walked straight out in front of me. He'd come from the field behind. His head was down, nose to the earth. I kept perfectly still. But then he turned and spotted me. He didn't move; he just looked directly at me. These animals are the last of the wild creatures. Like badgers, they are shy and will keep away from us. In that moment, it felt like a wonder and a privilege to enter his territory and be looked upon with those keen eyes. As quickly as he'd arrived, he darted away, not expecting to see anyone in his nocturnal kingdom.

The lights were on in the house, guiding my way through the gloaming as I ran inside to tell Richard and the boys about my encounter with the fox. The boys know I love foxes. For birthdays, my cards will invariably have foxes. I don't know if I've ever told them why; that these creatures are like signs from the world that life goes on, that nature replenishes itself, that there's hope after heartbreak, that perhaps souls can pass to the wild things.

When we moved to Donegal, one of the things I wanted to do was to keep hens. When I was a child, my maternal grandmother kept hens. My job, when we stayed with her, was to collect the eggs. It's still one of my favourite childhood memories. If I close my eyes, I'm back at the henhouse door. It's dark and cosy warm in here. The smell is earthy and of something else more pungent too, but not unpleasant. The hens are roosting and the straw smells sweet. To my mind, there was something miraculous about this place and I marvelled at it. The most magical thing of all was putting your hand underneath the chicken and finding the wonder of an egg, still warm to the touch. I would walk with it proudly in my hand across the yard to bring it to Granny Carey who would receive it with reverence, even though she collected the eggs every day.

Before we left Dublin, I bought a book on keeping ducks and hens, but the more I looked at it, the more I realised that my love affair with the fox would be called into question if we brought chickens here. I remember plainly my grandmother's distraught face when a fox got into the henhouse once. He didn't just take one. He killed them all, and the sight of her beloved chickens lying butchered was harrowing for her. Even though I cleared out a small shed purely for the purposes of a chicken coop, unless someone can make sure it's fox proof I'm not sure I can ever do it. They mean so much to me that I don't want to view them in a different way.

But it wasn't just foxes. I looked for signs everywhere. Signs of what exactly? I don't know. Signs that I would have another baby? Signs that my heart would heal, that the world was turning exactly as it should?

I don't know when my habit of gathering stones and shells started. It feels like I'd been doing this for a lifetime, but I also know that somewhere along the way the act of gathering took on more significance. It became a way of remembering, an act of honouring.

Treasures and totems, memorial stones, signs of life – you name it. I've gathered hundreds, perhaps thousands over the years. Every time I'd go to a beach, I'd load my pockets with pebbles and sea glass and a bright, clear stone. Some I'd use as memorials to the babies I'd lost. It was as if I was saying, 'You couldn't come on this walk but look, see what I've brought you back.' It was an exercise in remembering. These little offerings were me acknowledging that 'you' existed. It was my way of saying: 'You were a part of our family and this stone is my way of remembering you.'

These stones would go in my pocket, held deep inside for me to worry between my fingers and to bring home. But I gathered so many, I forgot where they came from. Sometimes I'd put them on Pio's grave. Sometimes I'd have so many I'd empty handfuls onto the little slate gravestone in the back garden. Every now and then, I'd have to etch that tiny little name onto the slate with one of the stones from my pockets. Three little letters that held so much sadness.

Sometimes I'd go to put on a jacket and find its pockets full of stones. I'd take them out and look at them and for the life of me I couldn't remember where they came from.

One year, on holidays, when I was still desperately trying to get pregnant and stay pregnant, I decided to book an expensive acupuncture appointment with a practitioner who was considered an expert in fertility. He was kind and patient, had trained in China and was so perceptive about what was going on for me that I almost wanted to run away. Almost – it was so expensive that I wasn't going anywhere until I'd received my treatment.

We talked, this stranger and I. He told me he perceived a certain sadness in me, that it was almost like I carried little stones of sadness around with me and guarded them like treasure. Tears sprang to my eyes, not out of sadness, but because sometimes a stranger can name something that you don't know how to yourself.

He saw it for what it was. I was gathering, storing and carrying pieces of sadness within me. To each of them I had temporarily granted a sort of power, a power to lessen my grief, to ward off evil spirits, to bring joy or luck and even to help. But they weren't lightening the load.

I have read about fertility stones, stones that women will traverse the earth to touch in the hope of having a baby. I would not have considered myself one of those women. But I had granted these stones a kind of power over me. Is that not the same thing? Some of them were little memorials to my lost loves, the ones who couldn't make it. The others were for me. They felt solid in my hand. I needed solid when so much felt uncertain.

The words of the acupuncturist made me feel not that this was futile – he wasn't judging me, he didn't even know of my habit – but that perhaps what I was storing was sadness itself. These little stones were allowing me to keep holding, not hope but sadness. And I didn't want to keep holding sadness anymore. I wanted to set myself free from something that was bearing down on me.

When I came home that summer, I started to set free these little souvenirs I'd gathered. I'd find myself walking on a windswept beach lashed by the Atlantic and I'd reach into the folds of my coat and invariably they'd be there. I'd take them out, examine them one by one and give them back to the earth. This is a hard habit to break. Some of them were so exquisitely beautiful that I'd understand why I wanted to have them for myself. My instinct is still strong, to find the prettiest one on the beach and bring it home. Perhaps there's a magpie in all of us for beautiful stones on a beach walk. It's funny because I think I've passed the same instinct on to my sons. They will load the boot of the car up with rocks they've gathered from a day at the beach. But I let them have their stones. Theirs are not loaded with anything. They are not granting their stones any special powers.

I'm not even sure it's that unusual a habit. It's natural to want to make our memories more real. We want to make our experiences last, and taking a pebble from the beach or an unusual stone from the mountain track is all about trying to make the feeling of that time endure, literally to give it shape and make it concrete.

Over time, I've emptied numerous pockets and said goodbye to pretty pebbles lost at the bottom of a jacket unworn for some time. And at times it felt like a betrayal. I had gathered it to mark the spot where I'd buried a tiny being, a little person I'd longed for. I almost felt like I was throwing away something that belonged to that baby.

But gradually as I'd kept gathering, these stones had become heavy in my pockets. In the same way that grief weighs you down, my little talismans were bearing down heavily on me. I realised that keeping them wasn't about honouring the past and that freeing myself from their weight was a liberation.

Once I threw a handful of stones into Lough Foyle all

in one go. I'd found them in a jacket pocket and flung them as I walked. For a moment I hesitated, wondering if I could plunge into the water to retrieve them. Surely I'd know them; they were so pretty that I couldn't mistake them. I'd be bound to recognise them in the shallows.

But sometimes healing starts with letting go. These little treasures have gone back to the earth. They were never mine in the first place. I still stop to admire beautiful stones, calling my sons over to observe the shapes and colours. But I resist the urge to gather, to lift and press them into my pocket. I do feel lighter.

I understand that what I was trying to do was to make meaning from what had happened. It was an act of honouring these tiny precious lives. But if my habit was to gather and to store, I had to let them go to make space in my hands and heart for new things.

People use the phrase 'letting go' all the time. As if it's easy. Just 'let go'. If only it were that simple to unburden your heart. One day I found myself on a beach at Malin Head. It was on a road I'd never been down before. At the end of the road there was an old stile that you climbed over to gain access to the beach. The sea was wild and restless. I stayed atop the stile and watched the white sea horses chase one another angrily across the beach. It looked like they were racing, biting one another to get to the shoreline first.

A man and his wife were out walking and they explained to me that the stones on this beach were not just any old stones. Here, they told me, were precious stones. Opals and other semi-precious stones were hidden among the ordinary pebbles. I laughed to myself. Could I trust myself to explore here?

The man told me that he gathered the stones. He remembered the first time he came to this beach and still had the very first stone from that day. A kindred spirit, I wondered. He told me the stones were full of questions, and you gather them, and when you have the answers you can finally let them go. I wondered had he seen into my soul. Had he seen the magpie in me, greedy to gather these treasures, to seek from them some truth?

What he said made its own sense. Maybe the questioning was over; at least the question I'd been asking over and over again was no longer one I was asking. Maybe I released the stones when I found the answer to my own question. If I couldn't be happy without another baby, maybe I couldn't be happy. Being happy with life exactly as it is – that's the answer. It's not always easy. Your own expectations of could've and should've can get in the way but I have thrown the questions deep into the ocean and they've sunk without trace.

That day, after I said goodbye to the man and his wife, I wandered across the dark sand with its high bank of pebbles. And indeed the stones and pebbles here were a wonder in all the colours of the rainbow from iridescent green to sky blue. Some looked translucent, while others looked as if a bird had discarded its perfect oval eggs on the beach. I held them in my hand and returned them to the beach. I had yearned for so long for some sign in the world to tell me that I would heal, that I would have another baby, that my heart wouldn't always feel broken, that I wouldn't always feel broken.

But that day on the beach at Malin Head, I realised that all of my searching had brought me here, to this place, closer to my true self than I'd been for a long time. The searching for signs was marking my way back to myself. Like Hansel and Gretel in the woods, leaving pebbles to guide their way home, my stones have taken me on a circuitous journey inwards.

Once you've experienced miscarriage, it's like going through a door or crossing a rubicon: you can't go back. But the strange thing is now I wouldn't want to. Would I choose those losses for myself again? Would I choose to be back in a place where I'm wrung out and numb? No, of course not. Nobody would want to be in a place like that. But life goes only forward and I wouldn't exchange my life experiences for anyone else's. They've made me who I am.

For a long time, all I saw was miscarriage. I saw it in my

face and my body. They had left their scars physically and emotionally.

When I looked in the mirror, I saw the raw sadness and the disappointment in my own eyes looking back at me. My body felt like a foreigner. But the experiences have also given me things that I hold on to like gifts. They taught me about true kindness and what it means to open your heart to hope. I had hoped for so long and saw that hope dashed against the rocks. But do I stop hoping? No, now I hope for other things. I understand about heartbreak a little better. I hope I am a better listener and a more compassionate friend. I am certainly kinder to myself.

There's a saying that grief is the price we pay for love. Things didn't work out how we wanted them to. But in a strange way, I now see those experiences for what they were, part of my life. Not the biggest part, not everything, but part of it.

Those experiences are not something I want to be emptied of. I don't want to cast these feelings out because to do so would be to throw away some of the best parts of me. Strange to say best parts. But it's true. I know that my experiences have made me a better person. I would have kicked and screamed and flailed against this very sentence had I tried to write it even five years ago.

There's an old Chinese proverb that says: 'The man

who goes on a journey does not come back the same person.' These journeys I have been on have made me look deep into parts of myself and realise some things had to go. They have taught me to look inside myself and to follow my heart into the wild places to make sense of it all. Grief gave me permission to be my full self and give expression to it by doing what felt right.

Sometimes this has meant digging my feet in the soil and saying no, I'm not moving. Sometimes it's meant running hard and screaming into the wind. Sometimes it's meant gathering my stones and then letting them go.

Grief made me go into the cave and enter the darkness of myself. I stayed there a while and I sat in the quiet, dark red hurt of this place. I was in there for a long time; I know that now. Sometimes people I loved tried to enter this space and I lashed out at them. But then I came back out again, ready to face the world, excited about exploring life again and what it might look like. Things didn't go to plan. I should know better. Scratch the plan and begin again.

I still look for signs, by the way. I am the daughter of a superstitious mother, who is in turn the daughter of a very superstitious woman. I can no more turn my back on the deeply ingrained practices of my forebears than on my own name.

I still throw salt over my left shoulder. My sons laugh

at this so hard. I will never go under a ladder and I curse the sighting of the single magpie as I scour the skies to see another. I will never bring a single snowdrop into our home – only a small bunch – and on New Year's Day I always bring in a piece of turf or lump of coal with me. Don't ask me why. I'll need to ask my mother for she passed these little habits on to me, which were in turn passed on to her. I will never look at the light of the full moon out of the window. Instead, I will go outside and stand and look at her and bask in her glow from my garden.

I keep an eye out for foxes still. One summer night not long ago, I got up out of bed for a glass of water. The moon was high in the sky and I could see it reflected in Lough Foyle. On the lawn in front of the house, a fox was walking, nose close to the grass that had been freshly cut. I don't know what he was doing. He seemed to stop every now and then, eat something and then move on. Even though no lights were on, every now and then he looked straight through the window at me, as if he sensed someone looking at him.

As he continued on in this way, he stopped, lay down on the lawn like a dog and looked up at the moon. This fox was enjoying his nocturnal travails so much that he actually looked up towards the moon. I could have watched him all night. He was so majestic in his movements, so sure-footed and yet cautious at the same time. I assembled everyone quickly and quietly, wanting to share this moment with my sleeping family. We all stood and watched him, whispering and wondering what exactly he was doing. And then he turned and looked at us. Did he recognise us from a different life?

A couple of springs ago, we put a night-vision camera in the woods. After much discussion about where it should go, Richard put it above a large hole in the ground near a rock at the edge of the woods. He strapped it to a tree and hoped that its infrared beam would yield some signs of the fox without disturbing its movements.

There are badgers' setts at the edge of the woods, but this one looked like a fox's hole, set apart on its own. There seemed to be another entrance to the hole nearby and so we left it alone for a couple of weeks.

We had been getting footage of the wild creatures in the woods with various success over the years. The badgers were plentiful and the foxes too, but the sight of a cub had eluded us. One morning, Richard slipped the digital card from the camera into the laptop and we all crowded around the screen for a look.

A cheer went up as a fox slipped out of the hole. A female, we assumed. Before too long, a cub crawled out. His fur was still dark and he was wobbly on his feet. He was swiftly followed by another. A third, a fourth and finally a fifth cub emerged from the hole. We were dumb-founded. It was like watching magic unfold. This beauti-ful little family living just right next door.

All these years I'd been looking, I realised, I'd been longing to see a cub. That would have been a sure sign that all would be well. I'd stopped looking and here they were – all five of them letting me know that life was unfolding exactly as it should.

CHAPTER 8

Dreams can be life rafts

In a dream, the two of us are walking through the field in front
of my childhood home.
In the distance Lough Foyle glistens under
the early evening sunlight.
The sun is dipping low and bright – so bright
I have to raise my hand to my eyes to look up at him.
We're walking slowly, idling even.
Nowhere to go, nowhere to be.
Just us, as comfortable in the silence as in speaking.
I raise my eyes to his face.
I hold his deep brown eyes in mine
and I feel a pure and complete love for him. I wake then.

This was a recurring dream that came to me long before I had my two sons. It seemed like a hyper-real kind of dream. Except in reality then I did not have a son. At that moment in my life, I did not have any children. But that dream felt sure to me and I knew that some day my son and I would walk the fields of my childhood home together.

In the dream, my homeplace was as familiar to him as it was to me. But in my day-to-day life, this place of childhood was far removed. It was hundreds of miles and a different lifetime away. When I tried to pick out the individual parts of the dream, they faded. I was like a child trying to grab hold of a butterfly, only to find the colours coming off like dust in my hands when I finally captured her.

This dream was like that: too delicate to touch with questioning thoughts. It all came apart in pieces that didn't make sense when I tried. Only the overall feeling of it remained tangible and I was as sure of it as I was of my own life. There was a question that came with it, like an itch that I couldn't seem to scratch. It was my own voice asking me: 'What would you do if you weren't afraid?' That's when I would wake and I did not know what that meant either. Not then anyway.

Many years passed and I found myself back in Donegal, grieving and questioning, and it was this question I was asking myself a lot. 'What would you do if you weren't afraid?' Afraid of what exactly? I was so afraid all of the time. By then I had two children and I had convinced myself that danger was never too far away.

Slowly but surely the boys built up their confidence and as time moved on, as is the way of things, they spent more time on their own. Off into the woods they'd go, disappearing for hours at a time. Their radius widened little by little. They would come in to me with cut knees, briar marks on arms, bruised shins, dirt covering their faces and hair. I would urge them to be more careful. Would I always be afraid? Is it a particular gift of motherhood to be more fearful of the world?

The world after miscarriage had become an unsafe place for me. I felt let down by life. I felt I had let myself and my family down. I was afraid of so many things, and so a kind of inertia had taken over. I remember sitting having a cup of tea at the kitchen table one day on my own, listening to the distant whirr of life, to traffic in the distance, the wall clock ticking, the fridge buzzing. It felt as if other people were doing something substantial with their lives, while I was sitting waiting for something that might never happen.

This path of wanting and longing for a baby is so lonely. Very few people in your life understand and you cut yourself off from people because it's just too hard. It's too hard to explain, too hard to feign happiness when someone you know announces a pregnancy. You don't want to be hurt anymore so you close up, like a snail retreating into its hard shell. You look out of your shell and you see people getting on with their lives and you're stuck, stagnating. But I've realised closing up doesn't protect your heart.

I had the sudden and stark realisation that I was fed up being afraid. I realised I controlled nothing. My thoughts were often like wild horses racing ahead on dangerously shifting sand and I was being pulled after them in a rickety wagon with the wheels coming off. Better to jump off and see what happened than be dragged to hell, I thought.

I picked up my keys and got in the car, knowing I was heading to the ocean. On this day, I felt a different energy rising. I had just moments earlier been sitting quietly and I had simply felt pulled to the sea. Inishowen is like the island of Ireland in miniature; the sea is literally all around us. Whatever direction you go, you will reach seawater, and on this day I felt the pull of the Atlantic.

I drove over Cnoc an Uininn, where the first signs of the big blue ocean can be seen. In the far distance, Culdaff Beach glimmers, the light reflecting off the white horses. 'To hell with being afraid,' a voice in my head said. I was so fed up being bashed by life's storms. I was fed up feeling I had to wrap myself in cotton wool. Pregnant, not pregnant, heal, try again, loss, surgery. The cycle had left my body a battleground and I was simply exhausted with the effort of it all. Richard and I had resigned ourselves to the fact that we couldn't do this anymore. We couldn't keep embarking on this journey any longer, but that allowed an unfathomable sadness to come in.

I pulled into the car park at Culdaff Beach. It's not unusual to have the beach to yourself and I followed the little wooden pathway to the sands. Even on a calm day, you know that this is a place of big, deep water and strong currents. The beach stretches as far as the eye can see. It's bound by rocks on one side and a river flowing into the ocean on the other. On this day, not a soul was in sight. It was so quiet that not even a footprint had embedded itself in the sand.

I started to peel off my clothes. I dropped them where they fell. I flung off my runners and jacket, dropping my leggings and T-shirt. If someone had come across these discarded items, God knows what they'd have thought.

But there's nobody around and it's a good thing too because I have no swimsuit. I strip to my underwear and keep walking. I couldn't care less if there was a cast of thousands on the beach. I just know I need to feel these waves. I want their energy. I want to get pummelled and thrown. I want to tell them to keep coming and I want to keep getting back up.

As I walked into the water, I could hear the words, 'What would you do if you weren't afraid?' ring out in my ears. It was my own voice that I could hear saying these words. The dream of many years ago, which I'd never forgotten, floated back to me in pieces. I could see my eldest son's brown eyes, the evening light dappling on the Foyle. And I was afraid. I was terrified. The further in I walked, the bigger the waves seemed. Being in among them was a different story to standing watching them from the safety of the beach. Soon the water was at hip height. Standing there, I could see the next wave building, gaining in strength and power. It would engulf me and the size of it was making me feel like I should head back into the shallows. As it approached, I steadied myself before diving under it.

Diving under a wave is a moment of pure feeling. It's not a thinking kind of moment. It's like a feeling of being swallowed whole. The sound is muffled. You are in the middle of something you can't control, something that feels a bit like a large and powerful jaw. You don't know which way's up or which way's down. The wave passed and my head broke the surface. I took a deep breath and swam to meet the next one. I reached it before it broke and was lifted feet into the air as it crested and smashed just behind me, closer to the beach. Even though I wasn't very far out – barely out of my depth – the power of the waves was enormous and, yes, I was afraid. While I knew I wasn't going to get carried away, the mind only sees the next wave coming. At no point did I put myself in any real danger, but the fight-or-flight stimulus awakened by the waves was enough to make me feel like I was tackling a beast.

My heart was pumping hard, but in those moments I felt so alive. As the water glistened on my skin, I wasn't grieving. I wasn't feeling sad. I was living in the moment, and in that moment in those waves I felt good. It felt good to be here in this beautiful place, immersed in cold water and drenched. I ran out of the waves, my body tingling, my skin pink all over. The salt water ran off my skin in rivulets down my face and out of my ears. I could feel myself smiling. I looked back at the ocean and gazed at it in awe. I'd been in there. For a few moments, I'd been tossed by its might. I'd been pummelled. Something of its deep energy still thrummed in my veins. I was part of this vast cycle of life. I couldn't control what had happened to me any more than I could stop a wave from crashing into me. The correlation of the two was immensely comforting to me even as I stood there all alone on the beach. I didn't feel lonely. I felt happy in my solitude. Happy to have had this experience by myself.

You can't stop the tide. Why would you want to? The wildness of this day infused itself into me. I wanted more of this feeling. I wanted to find more of that wild and to live it if not every day, then as many days as I could. I looked at the ocean again. Was it my imagination or did it look calmer now? The sunlight glinted on its surface. The waves looked like playful pups rather than angry lions. I smiled to myself, imagining that it had put on a show for me. It was exactly what I needed. The ocean had scared me, but it had also made me feel happier than I'd been by myself or with myself for a long time. I said thank you to the great vast ocean as another wave lapped at my feet. A peace offering, an invitation to return. I will always return, I promised the ocean that day.

I made that promise quite a few years ago now and it's one I have honoured as many times a week as I can. So many people came to the ocean or rivers or lakes in lockdown during the pandemic. Water became a balm in a world where life was untrustworthy. I felt like that too. Miscarriage had left its scars. I was waging a battle with my body, which I felt had tricked me and failed me.

How many times have I entered the ocean to find exactly what I've needed? My tears have joined with the vast ocean, salt water meeting salt water. In this place I've found an acceptance of myself.

I'm blessed to live in a place where so many opportunities for 'wild' swimming are possible. In the boot of my car I always carry the basics needed for a swim. Togs and towel go wherever I go.

I swim when I am happy. I swim when I am sad. I swim for no other reason than my body longs for the feeling of cold water, the sharp intake of breath as cold water splashes against belly, and finally immersion in the deep. If I haven't been in the water for a few days, I feel achy with a need for it.

When my boys were little, I told them a story that I am actually a selkie, that to have them I needed to come to dry land and leave my selkie skin somewhere safe. They liked to think that they were part selkie too and belonged to the sea in their own way. They're bigger now and these tall tales still make them smile. But still they know that when I get itchy feet or I'm off-form that I'll be getting in the car to go for a dip. I have to answer the selkie part of me that grew up smelling the salt water.

The truth is, unbeknownst to myself, a metamorphosis was taking place within me while I swam. I may not have been growing a tail fin, but my relationship with my body, which I had viewed with distrust and suspicion, began to change. It wasn't an overnight feeling of acceptance, but I found that as I swam, my body and mind seemed to feel more at ease in one another's company. Perhaps it was being out of my comfort zone – the sea is still not my habitat regardless of the stories I'd tell my sons. But my body and mind began to work in harmony with one another. My strong legs kicked hard, my arms grew muscular from pulling through water, my belly – the battleground where I lost my babies – became toned from swim after swim after swim.

In the ocean as I swam, I wasn't thinking about the babies I'd lost. I wasn't thinking about whether I was a good-enough mother. I wasn't thinking about who I was letting down. I was thinking of the next stroke, of pulling one arm out of the water quickly before plunging it back in and pulling it through the brine. I was thinking about breathing and kicking hard. I was watching that I was going in the right direction, not too far out, minding to stay parallel to the shore and sighting rocks and markers.

Here I was asking my body to do a job for me and it didn't just do it well, it did it magnificently. I am a strong and powerful swimmer. My body reacts the minute it hits water. My legs kick as one to get going – it's called a mermaid kick – and then I'm off. Moving through, pulling, breathing, one breath at a time. Sometimes I marvel at this journey. I look at this metamorphosis of sorts and I realise how far again I've come from my old self. We've travelled quite a way, I say to this skin I've lived in a lifetime. It makes the selkie story seem not so outlandish, this transformation I've made.

Sometimes I lie on my back and float and look up at the sky before flipping around and swimming a little bit more. I feel the engine of my heart revving up and I give thanks for it. Swimming in cold water is testing and the heart has to pump hard. In the winter months, I won't stay in too long. Three strokes in and four strokes out as Richard likes to joke.

I realise that I'm not alone in these feelings of transformation. When I talk to friends I realise that swimming has brought to them an acceptance of their bodies too. For so many women, our bodies are our battlegrounds. They have appetites that need to be suppressed. They have wobbly bits that need to be hidden or at the very least supported or flattened with lycra. They have bits that hang where the magazines tell us they shouldn't. They have bits that droop and sag as motherhood, age and dwindling collagen supplies change us.

Life has buffeted many of us by its storms. No woman I know has been unscathed by life's ravages. Sometimes those ravages are physical. Most likely they're emotional and you might never know it if you passed her by on the street. But the scars are mapped on her heart.

Swimming has taught me an honesty with myself and others that I didn't have before it was a big part of my life. Standing at the water's edge with a strip of elastane separating your birthday suit from the world, you feel vulnerable but also powerful. I had always been shy about changing in front of others. I'd be behind a rock, carefully negotiating from towel to togs and back into dry clothes again. Something happens when you swim regularly. You don't care so much. It's not that I have taken to being a naturist – far from it – but I don't feel the shame about my body that I once did. That shame of failure, of my body not doing its job, led me to feel awkward and uncomfortable.

Now I see it for what it is. I feed it, I nurture it, I honour it by taking care of it and it responds in kind. When I take to the sea, it responds by being the most powerful version of my body that it can be. I am in awe of it for that and I thank it daily for doing a good job.

In my work, I have spoken to many women who've told me how their relationship with their bodies changed over the years and most particularly when they started swimming. There, in the company of other women on the beach, they shed inhibitions they'd gathered and held for a lifetime. The water gave them permission to be fully themselves and they embraced the feeling and kept going back for more.

Remarks made in a woman's youth can last a lifetime. Women's bodies are still the brunt of so many jokes, cat-calls and insults. These small and not-so-small woundings can stay with us forever. When will society realise that another woman's body is not its business? We are all different shapes and sizes. In the water, it doesn't matter what shape that body is. The ocean doesn't care a fig how your body moves through it and bodies of every colour, shape and size do this in their own unique way.

The miscarriages were something that had happened. They were out of my control. They were like bombs going off inside me. But what happened after when I waged a kind of war with my body was avoidable had I had the tools to manage it better. I didn't know how at the time. But I know now and I will never ever again be so unkind to the physical parts of myself that keep me moving and swimming and putting one foot in front of the other.

When we moved to Donegal, I had a dream of the sea becoming a bigger part of my life. I wanted living in Inishowen to mean that I experienced the sea in my everyday. I could never have imagined the impact it would have on me, how much I would fall in love with it.

That's not to say that I am reckless. There are days I go to the ocean and I take one look at it and say not today. Even if the togs are on under my clothes, I will stay on dry land if the sea reminds me that its power and ferocity are things I cannot take a chance on those days. Instead, I'll walk across the rocks and breathe in the briny air or watch the gulls. I know from endlessly watching gulls that there are days when they're not fishing, they are simply playing in the wind and waves. The cormorants do this too and on the wild days, I watch them in their habitat and wonder what it might be like to have feathers for a few moments and to wheel and dip over the sea.

These 'no-swim' days are just as important as the swim days and you never know what treasure you might uncover. On those days, I thank the ocean for its power and promise to return when she has calmed down.

I like to think of the ocean as having emotions, and anger is one of these. When the waves lash the shoreline and you can't distinguish grey sky from sea, I understand that this is the time to leave her in peace, to watch from a safe distance until her power is spent.

On the calm days, when there isn't a breath on the wind, entering the sea is like entering a different universe. You realise that life is all around you as a spider crab walks on the seabed as you swim overhead. Swimming over a kelp forest, tiny fish dart away while you stretch your arms out to touch them. The colours of the kelp – golden browns, greens, beautiful murky hues – spread out below you and it's hard to look away. Once I swam over the blades of long seagrass that seemed to reach out for my arms as I swam past. I imagined myself trying to escape from their clutches, swimming hard to get away. This universe calms me down and makes me happy every single time.

I realise one day as I walk the beach, watching the ceaseless movement of the sea, taking a break to sit down on rocks from time to time, that my sons are imitating my behaviour. I watch as they continue to do what I do, watching, and then taking a moment to look at the sun and the sea from the safe distance of a flat rock. I realise that I'm a mirror for them. We've brought them to this wild place. They embrace the wildness in themselves and this knowledge is another gift the ocean has brought me.

CHAPTER 9

Finding the wild in me

There is only this moment of pure feeling.

My salt-lashed skin smarts and my heart pumps.

This ocean has taught me how to be myself again.

It has reminded me of my true nature;

that I too have wild and calm,

deep raging currents and channels of stillness.

I get into the car and drive over the hill road to Carndonagh, crossing ancient blanket bog, before coming into the town where I went to secondary school. I take the high road out of Carndonagh and head in the direction of Ballyliffin, where the ocean soon comes into view. It's October now and the day is fine with no wind.

Somewhere in the deep belly of the Atlantic, a storm must've been whipping up because the waves at Pollan Bay, where I park the car, are giants.

It's not unusual to see waves of fifteen feet high here. I like to walk close to where the waves creep up the shore, where I can judge the height and depth of the big rollers. Close enough to get a feel for them but not too close. Sometimes I stop and imagine what it would be like to be a sea creature in among these beautiful blue-green waves. This particular October day, I walked and watched. I was in no hurry home. School wasn't out for hours so I had time to myself and I found myself going with the flow. The waves cast their spell, hypnotising me with their noise and beauty.

I watched the terns walking the shore and laughed at the speedy little legs of the sanderlings walking almost maniacally in unison before taking off in flight as I approached. I observed the gannets plunge into the deep, each wrapping its wings around its body before they pro-pelled themselves at breakneck speed into the waves. I saw the cormorants dip their sleek heads under a wave before rising again in a different spot. I always marvel at the courage and bravery of these birds. Buffeted by the surf, they look so at ease even if the sea is a tempest all around them.

Something began to loosen in me that day as I walked. I

opened my eyes to take in this vista. In front of me, Pollan Bay spread out, the ocean violently lashing the sand and pebbles. On the horizon, Glasheady Rock stood solemn with white horses dancing all around it. In the distance, I could see the remains of Carrickabraghy Castle and set my course to it.

Life had brought me to the edge of myself and here I was feeling like I was on the edge of the world. Inishowen can feel like that. Because it's a peninsula, the light changes constantly. You will always find a place to be by yourself.

The longer I spent in Inishowen, back home, the more I found that getting out into the big open spaces, especially by the sea, was deeply healing and nourishing in my life. Even if I spent only twenty minutes by the shore before the boys came in from school with all their stories of their day, I'd be a better mother, better company if I had taken some time to myself. I realise now that while there is definitely some of the extrovert in me, more and more I need to go to quiet places and immerse myself in nature to restore. Being back home brought this part of myself home to me again. I was moving closer to the wild girl I had once been.

I have also learned how to pay attention, to observe the signs of the seasons changing and to accept and look forward to them all. When I started looking, really opening my eyes to look, it felt as if there were fleeting moments of magic all around me in the natural world. For so long I'd been blind to what was right here under my nose. Grief had left me closed up, eyes unable to see what was right under my nose.

Eyes open again now, I can gaze at the endlessly changing skies and know from the way the gulls are wheeling that a storm is coming. It's like they sense the growing restlessness of the seas and their own energy levels ratchet up to match it. My energy is like that too.

There is no season I don't look forward to – all have their own beauty – and as the year unfolds I follow the signs of change that Mother Nature leaves for us. When January comes, I fret that there are no snowdrops in the places I know to look for them. I should know better by now. They always come, just not at a time of my choosing. And so it will be some day that I'm out for a walk that a tiny clutch of them will stop me in my tracks. There they are, their shy heads, hanging down. But don't be fooled; any plant that will dare to stick its head above ground when the snow and the frost are still around is hardier than it looks.

At the back of my grandmother's farm house in Greencastle, more snowdrops than I have ever seen since grew in abundance. It was a quiet, shady spot where a sea of them appeared in January. She left the farm when I was twelve and I dug up a bunch and planted it in my parents' garden at home. They have spread and now they make quite the beautiful sight. My mother and I always talk about them as if they are things of great wonder. We look at them, always enchanted that they've come to visit us again.

On the last day of winter, on 31 January by the traditional Irish calendar, Mammy will take to the fields to gather rushes to make St Brigid's crosses. She will patiently sit and make as many as thirty or forty crosses. Over the years, it's become a tradition to send them to friends and family. My mother has a handful on her list and my list seems to grow year on year. I am painfully slow at making these crosses that symbolise the juices of the earth starting to flow again. Mammy is patient and has to show me every year, her hands working the rushes beautifully into crosses she ties.

Early spring is my favourite time in the woods. You can literally feel the sap rising, the birds getting noisier and busier from early morning. I check on the progress of spring by watching the unfolding of the sycamore leaves. First they are tight green buds. The buds grow larger and finally the big leaf that is held inside begins to unfold. I look for the ferns unfurling. They remind me of shy children hiding before extending their fronds to the sky. I gently touch my hand to the catkins dangling from the alders and watch as tiny green berries begin to form on the bilberry bushes. Come July they'll be bursting with fruit.

Each morning my feet tread the same path from the back door to the woods. I take my shoes off as I cross the garden, stopping to examine the sycamores, before I walk up the stone steps and into the woods. The same path brings something different into view each day. Now my eyes are open to the tiny changes that a day brings. Some mornings I might see the heron in flight following the path of the river to the Foyle. My boys long to find his nest in the woods, but he's secretive and I daresay his shelter is in some ancient tree near the waterfall.

One morning, I came upon a bees' nest. It looked like a badger had raided it in the early hours of the morning. Only a few honey bees flew around forlornly, their home desecrated by large hungry paws. Some days I will see signs of these big creatures that live in the woods, mushrooms upended or dug out, but I have never seen one in the woods in daylight.

Each day I sit and listen and watch as the trees in the woods transform in the springtime. It's a slow transformation, from naked branches to green foliage everywhere, and it is miraculous. My sitting-spot in the woods overlooks the deep gorge into the river below. From here my oak tree with the twin boughs rises up right in front of me. It has become my habit to end my vigil by stretching my arms up into the sky in unison with its stance. It is a way of saying I am once again open to the world, that

I will reach out my open arms and try to spend this day with a heart full.

There have been days when I've sat at this spot and cried into the earth, the same earth from which oaks take sustenance. They have sustained me too with their silence and their strength. When my heart was low and I felt empty with nothing to give them, their very act of extending their branches into the sky gave me hope. These strong branches reaching upwards, stretching out and up, was an act of hope. By my stretching out, I remind myself I am also nature and I too belong in this place.

Every winter in Inishowen wild geese from Greenland arrive. On many occasions we've heard them flying over our house as they come back to us. We've also watched them leave to head for their breeding grounds once again. One day last winter I was in Malin Head at the beach known for its beautifully coloured stones and I heard a noise that I thought was a pack of pups whelping.

I climbed the steep bank of the field above and there they were. Hundreds of Barnacle geese foraging in the field. I marvelled at these big birds coming all this way. Many of those that leave Greenland to winter in Europe stop on the Scottish Islands. Some venture across the sea to Inishowen and to Malin Head, the island of Ireland's most northerly point.

As I returned to the beach I had a strange encounter.

One goose was by itself and it just looked at me as I approached. I didn't want to scare it off so I sat down. It continued to observe me and came closer. I inched closer until I could reach out and touch it. The goose eyed me but allowed me to brush my hand over its soft feathers. When I told a birding expert of my encounter, he was suspicious of this interaction. I couldn't believe it myself, but sometimes when you least expect it, a wild creature will allow you into its orbit and you come closer to that wild magic that they possess.

I live about forty minutes from Malin Head and to me this part of the world is as wild and wonderful as it gets. The seas are rougher, the cliffs higher and more precipitous, the skies bigger, the hills bluer. You never know what you'll see here. In early March last year I sat looking out over the ocean from near Banba's Crown, at the extreme north, and a pod of dolphins swam past.

I've lost count of the number of times I've been in or near water when dolphins or porpoises swim by. I am always overawed by the majesty of these creatures as they move. I am grateful to live in a part of the world where I can witness their journey throughout the seasons.

A friend has told me she spotted an orca off Culdaff recently. It was identified because of the shape of one of its fins. Even if I can't see them, I love to picture these giants of the ocean somewhere in the deep, passing by as we bathe in the relative shallows.

From April we'll be watching out for the first sign of bluebells. Usually one of the boys will come into the house and tell me he's seen one. This is not a trivial statement in our house and the one who heralds the arrival of the bluebell must take me to the site at once. These flowers bring me so much joy. As soon as one appears, others quickly follow and by May the forest floor is a sea of blue. When my friend's beloved mother-in-law died suddenly one May, I brought a whole bunch of them as I couldn't think of what else to do to comfort her. These flowers brought so much soothing to her and her husband's heart that they've become totems of love and remembrance in her home. I try to remember to bring a bunch every year.

As the light fades in those early weeks of summer, the bluebells seem to infuse the whole woods with an inky hue. It's like an indigo mist descends on the woods and with it the most beautiful scent. They are like magic, and even though I welcome every season I feel a little bit sad as they start to fade. If you've ever noticed bluebells, they don't so much wilt as have the bright blue colour in their petals leech out of them. Then they go to seed.

But where one light fades, another glows and we know that the swallows will come soon. I watch out for them, but when you're not looking, there they are, swooping and dipping over the garden. Swallows build homes in our shed at the back of the house, making the most intricate nests. The shed ceiling is low, giving us a good look at them, but we don't visit too often for fear it'll put the birds off and they'll abandon their nests. I do shed a tear every year when I see them leave. It means the end of summer is coming, and I think of the perilous journey they have to make before they come back to us again. But they always return.

The space around our home is quite big, but I wouldn't call it a garden. It's left pretty much to its own devices, although we have planted wildflowers along the banks of the river and in boxes along the wall that separates our house from our neighbours'. These bring the bees and their flashes of exuberant colours give us a lot of joy.

A few years ago we asked a neighbour of ours if he minded us clearing a patch of rough ground opposite our house. We had the idea to plant a wildflower meadow. A good friend of ours with a digger dug out the overgrown bramble. We did our best to lift as many rocks as we could. We raked it over and prepared it and Richard bought bags of wildflower seeds.

There's a photograph I love of Oirghiall and me standing in our wellington boots, rakes held aloft, happy the job is done and we are ready for seeding. Once cleared, the space looked big and open. It would make a fine spot for wildflowers. And so we dipped our hands into big buckets of seeds and flung them far and wide, trying to distribute them evenly. We raked some dirt over the seeds so the birds couldn't feast on our work and hoped for the best.

That May, just as we were taking heart that the heads of some flowers had started to appear, we got a call in the middle of the night that would change our lives forever. Just before 4 am, I awoke to my phone ringing. I took the buzzing phone out of the bedroom and into the sitting room so I wouldn't wake Richard. How do you wake your sleeping husband knowing that what you are about to tell him will hurt him like nothing else ever has – that his younger brother, Davy, had died by suicide.

I went back into the bedroom where Richard lay deep in sleep. For some reason he'd switched his phone off that night. I looked at him in the darkened room lit up by the the bathroom light we always leave on for the boys in case they need to get up in the middle of the night. He looked so peaceful. I was going to disturb that peace with words that nobody would ever want to hear. I thought I was going to vomit. How do you make the shape of words like that? But I had to tell him. I switched on the bedside light and softly said, 'Wake up, love.' I needed him to be fully awake. I repeated these words until he was sitting up, the pillow propped up behind him. I told him I was sorry to wake him, that the news was bad, that Davy was dead.

Six months later, Richard's mother, Betty, died. This is the fact of it, but no words on a page can convey how much even writing these words still hurts. Betty was loved by everyone and she had a way of making everything beautiful. Where she was, beauty and kindness were. In her home, you felt loved and cherished. Sitting at her kitchen table, drinking tea and chatting were treasured times. I can't believe there won't be any more cups of tea with her and there won't be a time in my life when I don't long for that. When I think back to all the nights we stayed in Richard's childhood home, when Betty would peak around the door to say goodnight to us all, I am overwhelmed with the feelings of loss and love. But I try to hold on to the feelings she brought; feelings of being enveloped in love, care and comfort. On dark winter's nights we'd pull into the yard and the house would be glowing. Betty was like that. She glowed.

Her quiet wisdom was a gift. Her energy and enthusiasm for life were remarkable. She saw the good in everyone. I was privileged to have her as my mother-in-law. Truthfully, it is still hard to fathom that she is gone, this woman who was a light in all our lives.

In the space of two years, Richard lost his brother, his mother and a year later his father, Noel. Grief weighed heavily on us again. I am conscious that no telling of our lives in Donegal could be complete without speaking of their deaths. There are many people still grieving these recent losses and making sense of what happened and I'm also conscious that this isn't really my story to tell. It's enough to say that our hearts were broken all over again. It was a huge comfort to Richard when the summer after his mother died the wildflower garden bloomed. Betty could make anything grow and seeing this little space flourish felt like her telling us we'd be OK.

Davy was probably the handiest person I've ever met – there was nothing he couldn't make, do or mend. He made the most beautiful treehouses. If we were ever passing by a house with a treehouse in the garden, Dallan and Oirghiall would take a look and say: 'Nah, not as good as Davy's.' It was true. The treehouses he built were works of art.

When Richard started watching YouTube videos of master treehouse builders, I hadn't a clue what he was planning. Slowly but surely he put together his own construction and it is a wonder. The platform is built around the trunk of a sturdy oak in the woods, with wooden planks buried into the ground holding it up. It has a trap door and a ladder and a balcony made of painted driftwood. It even has a tarpaulin tied between trees that makes it look like it's sailing above the river. The boys go there to hang out, and some sunny evenings Richard and I bring two glasses and a bottle of Prosecco and sit there.

It's a monument to a man we loved very much. I think he'd be proud of what his big brother, who'd never built anything like this before in his life, has made.

In the darkness of the winter after Betty died, life seemed to have shrivelled and lost its colour. Just before Christmas that year I was sent on an assignment to the ISPCA regional centre outside Letterkenny to do a piece with the seasonal message reminding people that a dog is for life, not just for Christmas. That day the heating system in the boys' school was broken and I rang the ISPCA centre to see if it would be OK if my children tagged along. At the door of the centre we were met by the manager, Denise, holding a collie pup in her arms. The alarm bells started to go off in my head. The boys, who had already been begging us for a dog, were going to go into overdrive now.

The thing is it wasn't really the boys. As Denise walked towards us, carrying this little black and white bundle in her arms, I felt something crack in my heart. It was an actual sound. My first dog had been a collie. Jim had had a collie for many years of my childhood. They have always been my favourite dogs. They were also Richard's favourite kind of dog too. 'Oh, no we're in trouble now,' I said to myself. I left after doing all my interviews and talking to the staff and meeting the canine inhabitants, promising that we'd be back in touch. That weekend we returned to the centre for Richard to meet this small dog who had grabbed a hold of my heart. 'What do you think of him?' I asked. We were both so heartbroken that the thought of taking in this pup felt like it would be healing for all of us. Richard nodded his assent. He literally couldn't speak. The dog had cast his spell over him too. A few days later, we brought him home. We call him Wyatt and while he loves all of us, he loves Richard best and is most content when curled up at night by his feet.

Sometimes in our little place it feels as if nature could soon take over if we were absent for any length of time. When Richard was cutting back a hedge one evening, he found that scores of wasps were entering a hole right where he had been working. On closer inspection, he noticed that throngs of them were going in and out. We had to call an exterminator who arrived with a hazmat suit, ordered us indoors and told us he'd never seen so many wasps in one nest.

Living beside a river has the effect of soothing you and bringing wild creatures to our door. The swallows love to swoop along its surface catching flies, and dragonflies, with their lustrous blue bodies, dance around in summer. But sometimes we are also reminded – if I needed reminding – that we're not in control and nature can unleash a ravenous and dark side too.

In the summer of 2017 as we returned home from our

holidays, it began to rain. We joked in the car that we hadn't seen rain in weeks and here we were back in Donegal and it was torrential.

We ran from the car into the house, soaked in a matter of seconds. This rain felt different. My great-aunt Maggie had so many ways of describing rain and I don't know if even she'd have had the vocabulary for this sort. I joked that this was the kind of rain she'd call 'a thunder plump' but this one seemed biblical.

From early evening it kept raining hard and heavy with flashes of lightning forking in the sky. Richard put on a raincoat and went up the woods. He came back in ashen-faced as he said it was like a raging torrent coming down the river valley. The Drung river started to rise and it kept rising.

All over Inishowen, bridges fell, banks slid and water levels rose. Flood waters ripped into people's homes. We could only watch in horror as our river, this beautiful passive force in our lives, turned into a raging beast. We tried to shore up some makeshift defences, lifting anything heavy we could find to stem the flow of water that was coming closer to the house. One of the things that made it worse was that the high tide coincided with the peak of the rainfall. There was nowhere for the water to go and we could only watch and see what happened. With the boys safely in the house, we heard a crack at the back of the river. The holly tree that had stood there for decades was snapped like a match and carried away in the torrent.

When I was a child, it was my job to gather holly for Christmas. Each year I'd climb this tree and pick holly leaves with the brightest berries to adorn our home. Now I could only watch as it was carried off at speed. Just moments later, a huge ancient-looking tree flew past. We worried that if it hit the bridge too hard the bridge would collapse, and then if the water backed up even further we'd really be in trouble. We were lucky, but others all over Inishowen weren't so lucky, and the floods of that August night in 2017 were devastating.

Some weeks later, Richard noticed something lying along the shoreline. We knew it was a tree and he went over to inspect it. The holly tree we'd lost was lying there, washed up by the tide. A strong ivy casing had covered the tree, wrapping around it in an intricate lattice, and this had separated itself from the tree. We dried it off and brought it inside. It is like a piece of sculpture, otherworldly and very beautiful. Everyone who sees it admires it and we have hung tiny fairy lights on it to show it off. It reminds us every day that we are passing through; that nature is fierce and we are only minding this place for the next generation.

For me, our home extends outwards in the summer. We are outside more than we are in. My boys dispense with shoes to run through the woods barefoot and I laugh because I was no different when I was their age. The long summer nights are for adventuring and as often as we can, we pack the car and pitch a tent.

For weeks we'll have been gathering and hiding firewood at Kinnagoe Bay ready for our night under the stars. We walk to the second beach and begin the task of assembling our home for the night.

Richard and I have camped in the Andes and by the banks of a river in Alaska. We camped in the Macgillycuddy Reeks in Kerry and in Swiss Alpine valleys. But there's nowhere like Kinnagoe Bay when the sun dips and you fall asleep to the sound of the waves.

It was on this beach that many years ago Richard and I wondered if we could make a life work in Donegal. It always strikes me as something beautiful when I watch our two sons with their dad around our campfire.

On one particularly memorable night as we watched the last flames of the fire die, a lone kayaker swept past in the almost-dark. He looked surreal, the only sound his paddles dipping into the sea. A seal popped its head up out of the water and I saw that it was eating a fish. The stars came out and we told our stories and laughed at how Richard and I always seem to have the same row over putting the tent up.

Despite all the beautiful places I've been lucky enough

to visit in my life through travel and work, the comfort I feel in a tent at the edge of Kinnagoe Bay on the edge of Inishowen on the edge of this country is immense. There, as the four of us fall asleep with the ebb and flow of the Atlantic in our ears, I realise that this is the place in the world I feel happiest.

Underneath the sheet of fabric in a sleeping bag with the three people I love most in the world as the stars shine down on us outside under a bright moon if we're lucky, I feel complete and utter gratitude for everything that has brought me to this place and everything that's happened along the way. All that has passed along the way has only solidified my sense of being thankful for this time with these people I love in this wild and beautiful place.

All of these things and adventures helped me to fall back in love with my life. They made me realise that nature is all around us. It can be cruel and wonderful, all in the same day. The only thing we can do is embrace each day and try to live with as much love as we can because that's really all that's important at the end of the day.

CHAPTER 10

You always saw me

'The time to be happy is now,
the place to be happy is here.'
You wrote this on my fortieth birthday card.
It took me a while to realise it –
I'm glad you never forgot.

I can remember a few years ago waking early in the Swiss Alps at the home of my sister-in-law to the sound of a baby crying. It was the first time I had heard a baby cry loudly and it did not hurt. Was I healed?

What does that even mean? If it means it's no longer painful to think of what might have been, then no, I'll never be 'healed'. But if it means that I can hold my pain and it doesn't crack open my heart, then perhaps I'm going in the right direction. Nobody gets everything they want in this life.

My sister-in-law, a very wise and caring woman, told me that life is about being happy with what you have. That's the secret. I had chosen to believe it was about chasing after something else. I know better now.

Over the years I had run so hard to heal. I had tried many things to get pregnant and stay pregnant. I had cried and listened to advice and prayed. I had looked in many of the wrong places for answers to what was happening. I had looked into the eyes of doctors, shamans, priests, gurus and all kinds of practitioners of wackery. As well as genuine professionals, there are snake-oil salesmen on every journey in life, and the fertility journey is a place where they pop up all over the Yellow Brick Road.

I'm sure that some can smell your desperation at a hundred paces. They say, 'Don't worry, we'll get you pregnant.' This sounds laughable and yet you believe it and you hand over your money. You believe it because you're so tired and hurt and you'll try anything once. I had just wanted someone to tell me it'll be OK, that they could see into their crystal ball and it was all going to be fine.

I had sat in rooms, lain on tables as hands were laid on me and I had asked healers of all creeds and none to work their magic. As I was asking them all of these questions, I had stopped asking the one person who always saw me warts and all, for his thoughts. I was in such pain at constant loss that I had stopped asking the one person who knew and loved me best what he thought: my husband.

After all those years of loss, there came a time when we knew we'd reached the end of the line of trying for another baby. We couldn't keep doing that anymore. Even I had realised that this was torture. But how do you say enough, no more when for so long it's all that's consumed you? I'm no expert but I think we were spent and while we loved one another very much, there was a limit to how much any couple can keep going.

It pains me to write this now but there was a time when Richard and I were drifting in our own orbits. The constant cycle of pregnancy and loss had taken its toll on us.

We were communicating with one another of course, but it was on a superficial level. For Richard and me, who'd never stopped talking, here we were like planets in our own separate solar systems floating all alone in a lonely space. What's worse is that I didn't see it happening. I was just busy, busy, busy. Better keep busy. Keep going, don't stop.

Now I can see that he was trying to let me burn myself out. He was patiently watching me like a Catherine wheel, whizzing around and around, before eventually fizzing to a stop. But when I get going, I can go a long time without stopping. I've always been a bit of an insomniac. I can get by on little sleep and I will push myself until I fall over.

I had kept papering over the cracks that were appearing. We were fine. The kids were fine. We were managing fine. The boys were happy. Dinner was on the table. I'd been taking on some more paid work. I was training for triathlons, for God's sake. But I had never alighted for long enough in one place to acknowledge what was going on between us.

I understand that I couldn't bear to think or even talk about Richard's pain. Even writing this is hard. For it was painful for him. He had hopes and dreams of our third child too. He's told me that the miscarriages caught him off guard, that he never saw them coming or the impact they would have on our family. He watched the woman he loved turn into an obsessive, raging beast

I couldn't ask him how he felt because I was just too sad. I was having a hard time dealing with my own grief and if he had told me how he was feeling, it would have tipped me over the edge. It sounds ridiculous not to talk about something so fundamental. Yes, we talked about it in vague superficial ways but not really. Perhaps I was afraid that if I really heard his pain, it would increase the feelings of failure I already carried and that would have sent me off the deep end.

So many years have passed and we never had our much-longed-for third child. You must also know that we're OK, that we found one another again and with our broken hearts we turned to one another again.

I understand that in trying to find answers and healing from the hurt I carried, I searched in some of the wrong places. I searched in some of the right places too and in the company of good friends, I made a lot of sense of things.

But the one I needed most, I turned away from. We stopped talking about what was deeply in our hearts. We were angry at one another and hurt. No, I've said that wrong. I was angry at the world and Richard bore the brunt of it. As time went on and I continued to go at breakneck speed through life, I know there were many times he felt angry with me too and hurt that I seemed to choose the company of friends and acquaintances over him. I was literally running from our home rather than choosing to sit and talk.

I am so sorry I stopped talking. Thankfully, it wasn't too late to mend things. I realise mostly that my clever, sensitive and kind husband saw through me most of the time. When I didn't want to see what was really going on, he always saw it and he never stopped seeing me.

He saw me every single day and he waited patiently for me to burn myself out from running around trying to fix myself. There's no fixing to be done, I realise that now. Just time and patience and a lot of love. I'm lucky he gave me all that.

I got to the point where I knew it was time to stop running. I would look at the trees in the woods and wonder what it was like to be so strong. I had become a will o' the wisp, flying here and there and landing everywhere but never long enough to settle in. I got so tired of doing, of being, of becoming. It's not a race. The one person driving me was me and I was a hard task master.

I had convinced myself that if I could try one more thing or achieve one more goal, then maybe the stars would align. My body hurt so much from wanting and trying to have another baby. My womb ached from the longing. It was an actual pain. My heart throbbed with an unceasing restlessness that wouldn't allow me to sit still. My brain was frazzled from overthinking. It was like my head was full of moths, all flapping around. Thoughts of another child were the lamplight that suffocated all the light to think of anything else. My back hurt, my head hurt. Was there a part of me that didn't hurt?

So what changed? I think we started talking to one another again, Richard and I. I was no longer running from his pain. It hurt me to let it in but it was the first step to me returning to us.

I had my stories, but he had his: stories that I hadn't even been aware of. He told me that the day after we'd buried Pio in the back garden, he found himself at a work event in Dublin. It was a commitment he had to honour. In the middle of this event in a room full of movers and shakers, he looked down and saw his shoes. The soles still had mud from the garden where we'd dug a tiny little hole for a tiny little person.

This story broke my heart all over again. His pain racked me with guilt for walking away from it, for not acknowledging it for so long. We were still us. Before we had our children, I'd felt like we were always enough, like he was my family, my sun, my moon, my stars. How had I allowed myself to stop seeing him?

The truth is we do strange things when we're hurt. We run away. We hide. We dig a hole. We disappear into drink or drugs or someone else's arms. I was just running but a bit like a headless chicken, I never seemed to get anywhere. I realised it was time to stop running, that whatever I needed wasn't going to be found outside the four walls of my home. It needed to start with me and I needed to come home to myself and to my husband.

Just stop striving, stop running, stop trying, stop caring so much, stop competing, stop wanting, stop hurting, just stop. It was time to find a new path, a new way of being a couple again without the burden of constantly trying for another baby.

I haven't got this sussed. Relationships change. I've known Richard since I was twenty-three years old. That was more than half my life ago. I realise that when we got married we knew very little about what life had in store. We had lots of hopes, dreams and love. We still have lots of hopes, dreams and love. We've been hurt and we hurt one another, but I can honestly say there's nobody else I want to tell my stories to first. He still laughs at my jokes. We had to find a way back to one another and luckily we still cared enough to try.

It wasn't just about our children. We always chose us. On our wedding day one of the readings was from the Book of Ruth. We chose it because it was popular for weddings and we liked its meaning. I read it again recently. 'Wherever you go, I will go. Wherever you live, I will live. Your people will be my people.' Its words resonate even more deeply now than they did all those years ago.

Not long ago, one Valentine's Day, one of my editors asked me to talk to couples who had renewed their vows. One of the challenges of my work is finding people to talk to you, to tell you their story, to share it in an honest way to make it compelling for readers. I found two couples: one starting out on their married life and the other many years in like Richard and me.

I talked to them about what marriage meant and what they said resonated a lot. The older couple had no idea what life was going to throw at them when they started out. They'd had their own suffering to deal with and it struck me not for the first time, that marriage is more than anything else about finding someone to walk the path with you and finding someone to hold you when you are weighed down by life's burdens. You do the same for them and together you experience the ups and the downs that life brings.

Richard and I got married on a beautiful September day in 2000, surrounded by all our friends and family, in the church right beside where we live now. So many of those we loved are gone since then, but our sons were born and many nieces and nephews. That decision to say yes to him was beyond doubt the best of my life. There are things in life I'd undo or change, but I would never change that day.

We're not newlyweds now. We've known one another for what feels like a lifetime and yet we are still learning about one another. Our spark that I thought had been extinguished by loss came back. We have a habit of lighting the candle that was on the altar on our wedding day every 16 September, our wedding anniversary. We laugh as it sputters into life. If one of us is away, we will send the other a photo of the candle burning.

We have developed a habit of going for a swim on a Monday morning. It's one we try not to break and when we get the kids out to school we put our dog, Wyatt, in the car and head for the beach with a flask of hot coffee.

Winter swims are the ones I love most, mainly because we have the beach to ourselves. We sit in the car, sometimes watching the rain or hailstones bounce off the car's bonnet and laugh at the ridiculousness of deciding to take the plunge in this.

I try to cajole him that we could always leave it, that it wouldn't kill us just to sit in the car and drink the coffee and look out the window. That's his cue to tell me that he came here to swim. And so I take my towel and we head for our changing rock. I call it our changing rock as there's usually nobody else around on a Monday morning to claim it.

We are creatures of habit. I'm out of my clothes, swimsuit already on underneath, in a flash. Richard never rushes. I dance on the spot or do a length of the beach to warm up and brace myself for the cold. The poor dog watches this ritual with a mix of wonder and dread as he is left alone on the shore. He hates the waves.

If you ever watch people enter cold water, no two people do it the same way. I dance and flounce and shriek quite a bit. Richard walks purposefully in and then ducks under as a wave breaks, showing the bravery of a cormorant. I trail my fingers, letting the water rise higher and higher before succumbing to its icy grip, and then we swim.

In the coldest months, cold water feels like it's nipping at your muscles. It's like little bites under the water. We've got used to that feeling. We laugh and whoop and float on our backs. Some days the waves are so big and we just spend a while jumping to meet them. It's on those days I look at my husband and the years slip away. This is how we've always been.

The days when the water is calm, we'll stay in for a few minutes and float and have a chat. We never tire of this view, looking back to the beach and to the big lighthouse there, our dog waiting patiently by our piles of clothes for us to return.

Richard always gets out first. I stay a few extra minutes because I know it takes him ages to get changed and I'd rather be in the water than standing waiting for him. I watch him walk up the beach and realise how lucky I am to have found him. I also realise that I wouldn't change any of it, not one single thing. It brought us to this place of understanding one another, of knowing one another more deeply.

We dry off and if it's fine we'll drink our coffee on the beach and if it's Baltic we'll get in the car and shiver as we try to hold the cups straight and we'll laugh again as the rain pelts the car, heating turned up full blast. It's not everyone's idea of a date but for us it's priceless. It's the best way to start a Monday morning in the best of company. I wouldn't for the world trade those moments of sitting in the car looking at the ocean after a swim.

So if he were to ask me again to marry him, knowing what was in store, I'd say yes, a hundred times yes.

CHAPTER 11

The women and other lighthouses

You pour the coffee; I pour the tea,
and together we drink deeply of life's ups and downs.
Your heart has been dashed on the rocks
but you pick up the pieces
and the tapestry you've woven with those shards is dazzling.
My own heart – with all its broken bits and sharp edges –
is smoothed just by being in your orbit.

The lights of my friend Sinead's car tell me that she's at the gate. She wanted company to drive in the early hours of the morning to the place where we'll gather for Darkness into Light. There's something lonely about being on the road at that time of the morning, she told me the evening before as we made our plans.

I hop in the car with the boys, leaving Wyatt wondering why we're up and out in the middle of the night. We drive to Shroove Beach, listening to St *Elmo's Fire* by John Parr on the car stereo (the boys have recently discovered a penchant for eighties' music).

Shroove or Stroove – it's *An tSrúibh* in Irish so Stroove is probably more correct – is the small Atlantic cove past Greencastle where I've been coming since I was a teenager with my friends the two Marys, as we always called them, and Antoinette. Accessed by a sloping wooden pathway, it has a lighthouse at one end and rocks and an old stone diving board at the other end. Also known locally as the Big White Bay, it's become very popular with swimmers and dippers of all abilities. I dream about this place when I've been away from it for any length of time.

The beach is dark when we arrive, even though there's a line of pink on the horizon, telling us that the dawn we've risen to witness isn't too far away. My friend Geraldine – I can pick her out because she's the one wearing a camo dryrobe just like mine – is busy setting up battery-operated tea lights the length of the pathway to the beach. They light the way and seem like they've come from a fairy tale. How fitting it is, I think, that it's

Geraldine lighting our way. My beautiful friend lost her husband and her two children in a tragic car accident near the village of Quigley's Point in 2020. Here she is arranging lights to make the event more special. Then she's on the beach putting the finishing touches to her lights display and spelling the word 'Hope' in mini lights.

There's a lump in my throat that I swallow hard to get rid of. I want to take in this beautiful scene, the sight of people arriving, wrapped up against the wind. They say the darkest hour is just before the dawn. It certainly feels like it's the coldest when you've been roused from your sleep to come and stand on the open shore. The waves are crashing on the beach and the line of pink is now spreading to take over a small patch of the horizon in the distance. It's a deep pink at its centre, softening into lighter shades of pink and peach as it proliferates. It's so beautiful.

I think of Davy, Richard's brother, and what this sunrise might look like to him wherever he is. More people arrive on the beach. Someone lights a small campfire in a metal container. My two boys have taken charge of a bucket, asking people to throw in whatever coins they have. It's brightening and it's almost time to get into the sea. We take some photographs, lining up in our swimsuits and yellow T-shirts with the 'Darkness into Light' logo printed onto them.

And then we step into the tide, which is full, and we get

battered by the waves. They crash over our heads, into our ears and slap us in the face. But theirs is a playful energy today. It's not a force that would knock you over. Many friends have come together for the dip and to welcome the sun up.

I try to take stock, to feel all the feelings. Everywhere, in front of me, behind me, on the shoreline are women I know and love. My sister Anne-Marie is in the water. Her children are on the shore with mine. Some of my dearest friends are here, all of us being trounced by waves and laughing and trying to take some pictures before the next waves comes in. I feel at once with them and removed. The pink of the sky is still there, just a little bit now, but it's already dissolving into a dirty grey light. Faces are becoming more easily recognisable. Life could have been so different. If only Davy could've held on that fateful night when the pain of being alive was just too great. In this moment, I take comfort from the people on the shore and those in the water. I wish Richard could be here but his work commitments presenting a radio show on RTÉ every Saturday morning mean he cannot be with us.

I look at these women who've all shown up. This is my community of women. These are my people. I know every one of them. They've all come to mark Darkness into Light in their own way. Some are my closest friends. To think that a decade ago I didn't even know some of them. Can a heart be low and full of joy at the same time? I know that it can. Can it feel all the love and loss at once? Yes is the answer.

We dry off and I pour a hot chocolate for my friend Bridgeen and me. She's come from Burt, a good hour's drive away, to be with us. I introduce her to some of my more local friends. Some are sitting, warming up, drinking from steaming mugs of coffee and hot chocolate. There's a fullness to what I'm feeling. I don't feel the cold. The pink has leeched away and the magic glow cast by the candles is gone. But there's still something magical in the air, a feeling of solidarity woven by women coming together to support one another in this way for a worthy cause. I drive home and think of paths lit by candles and how friends showing up are like lights in the dark.

My mother had a saying when I was in school: 'Show me your friends and I'll tell you who you are.' She'd say this often to my sisters and me. It used to annoy the hell out of me. I had good friends but I felt she was putting us in a box. Now I see that there's wisdom in it because my friends are an eclectic bunch who don't fit into a homogenous group. Their gift to me is that in spending time with them, I've found out so much about them but also about myself.

I am the only woman in the family I created. I love these menfolk who make every day of my life better, but it's in the company of my friends and my sisters, Anne-Marie and Carol, that I've come to realise we have more in common than we have to separate us. This often low-level lunacy we sometimes feel about our lives is pretty much universal. These women have taught me that. We are all different shapes and sizes and ages. Some are mothers, some are not. We've come from different places. Our hearts have been battered, bruised and pulled apart in a million directions but when we come together it doesn't matter. We don't see the damage. We only see the beauty and the tenderness. These women – my mother, my friends, my two sisters – have been the lighthouses for me, guiding me home when I was at sea.

Back when I got into the sea at Culdaff that day all those years ago when I peeled off my clothes and headed straight into the water, I'd already been dreaming of how to make the ocean a bigger part of my life. Swimming and being pulled towards the ocean have brought so many friends into my life. It's opened so many new doors of discovery.

I don't know when I started noticing it or becoming curious about the lighthouse that stands conspicuously in the middle of Lough Foyle at Moville. The freestanding lighthouse is one of only three of a kind still surviving in Ireland. From the National Inventory of Architectural Heritage, I learned that it was originally erected in 1882 to mark the navigation channel along Lough Foyle from Derry to the south to the open seas to the north, which became a very busy route during the second half of the nineteenth century, with ships travelling to and from Derry. Once in the Atlantic Ocean, they'd make their way to America and Australia amongst other destinations.

It originally had a paraffin-powered light and, apparently, the keepers lived in Moville and rowed out and stayed on the lighthouse every night to ensure the light was maintained during the hours of darkness. To my eyes, it's incredibly beautiful.

I remember one Friday evening many years ago taking Dallan and Oirghiall for a fish supper in Moville. They were only tiny things eating their chips from soggy brown bags as we sat on one of the sheltered beaches along the shore front. The evening was cold and sharp and our chips cooled quickly. Looking out across Lough Foyle to the hulking outline of Binevenagh Mountain on the northern shores of the lough, the whole scene was like a painting. And if it was a painting, someone must've thought this beautiful view was not enough and added in a perfectly symmetrical lighthouse for dramatic effect.

Did anyone ever swim out there? Would that be something you could do? I wondered. How far would it be and wouldn't it be something to make it that far?

As it happened, there was an annual swim to the

lighthouse every year. It was an organised event. I'd even spoken to one or two people who'd done it. There were stories of dolphin encounters and of water so choppy the swimmers couldn't make it around the lighthouse and so just swam to it and back, avoiding a circumnavigation of the light. Sea charts show that just at the light the water level drops massively. The thought of an abyss underneath scared me and exhilarated me in equal measure. I'm terrified of really deep water.

For some reason, an idea formed in my brain. I would become a good-enough swimmer to make it to the lighthouse and back. But I was a long way off being able for a swim like that. As a child, I was always drawn to the water, but was never a great swimmer. Once when on a school outing I got in trouble at the local pool; a friend's mother had to jump in fully clothed to pull me out. To this day, the smell of chlorine triggers a memory of panic even though I am now a confident swimmer.

My first summer of college was spent on an island off the coast of Brittany. Île-de-Bréhat became my home for three months in the long, hot summer of 1992. I was a *stagiaire* – or intern. In return for lodgings and meals, thousands of students worked in hotels all over France. At the end of the summer, you got a few quid but it was tough work and largely unpaid. I'd gone to Bréhat because my mind got snared at the mention of lighthouses and beautiful sunsets. These *phares de Bretagne* inspired artists and photographers to come and look at them. As part of the requirement for taking a foreign language for your degree at Maynooth University, you had to spend six months in that country. Most language students spend the summers of first and second year abroad and so it was that I found myself on a plane to Paris having never been on a plane before and making my way to this island in 1992.

And it was in the waters off the island that I took my first tentative strokes as a swimmer. I was on Bréhat for the summer with another language student from May-nooth University, Mary. When her boyfriend Cathal came to the island for two weeks' holidays, he and I hung out together when Mary was working. Mary and I rarely had any time off together and I was glad of Cathal's company. I don't think I've have ever properly thanked him for teaching me to swim. He had the patience of a saint. When I arrived back from France, I could swim.

When I met Richard, he was swimming in the sea. During the first winter we were together, he was doing the whole swimming-through-the-winter thing. But back then, more than twenty-five years ago, swimming all winter long was for the brave or the mad.

He'd drive us to the Forty Foot at weekends and I'd take the plunge, but I never had the courage for the winter dips. I'd sit on the beach at Greystones at weekends while he jumped in with one of his old college friends. I'd laugh at the sight of the two of them trying to pluck up the courage to dive in.

When we moved to Donegal, I fixed my mind to making the lighthouse swim a reality and started driving to the local pool in Derry city a couple of mornings a week.

Starting a new life in a new place – I'd recommend going to the local pool. There's something about being in your togs along a tiled wall that breaks down barriers. After a few weeks of seeing the same faces at the pool, a group of women asked me to join them. Before I knew it, we were meeting for coffee. I am eternally grateful to Bridgeen Byrne, one of my closest friends now, for reaching out the hand of friendship. I jumped at the chance. Through that single encounter, doors opened and new friendships appeared. I signed up for an all ladies try-a-tri – a shortened version of a triathlon event. The training involved immersing ourselves in swimming and biking and running. I had to throw myself off the deep end in terms of new people too. I was making new friends – something that we all need to thrive in a new place.

I completed the try-a-tri, crossing the line red-faced and emotional, falling into the arms of my three biggest supporters – Richard, Dallan and Oirghiall. Crossing the finish line wasn't the end of the story. It marked a new beginning. I joined the local triathlon club and started swimming in club sessions a couple of times a week. A group of us decided that we'd car pool instead of driving three or four separate cars to the sessions. The conversations on the way there and back made it worth the effort.

Your improvements as a swimmer happen in tiny increments, so tiny as to be almost imperceptible. Over the years, I plugged away. I never missed a session. I took myself to the sea as many times a week as I could and always on a Monday with Richard. The pandemic, which saw the pools close, meant that if I wanted to continue to swim, it was going to have to be outdoors. I updated my wetsuit and decided to go the distance outdoors.

A few summers ago, with my friends Adrian Harkin, who runs a kayaking outfit in Moville, and the chef Brian McDermott, along with another friend Pearse Moore, the chief executive of Derry's Nerve Centre, I swam to Moville lighthouse and back. Richard and the boys provided my kayak support.

The day was perfect. The sun glistened off Lough Foyle as I eyed the lighthouse through my goggles. Finally, I was going to get a close-up of this light that had caught my eye many years earlier. I swam steadily, my eyes catching sight of my back-up crew as my head tilted to take in air. And there it was, standing tall and proud – my light. I'd made it.

Dallan's school-run journey takes me into Moville past the lighthouse every day. Its sure and steady presence is a focal point for my imagination. Memories of swimming beneath its gaze come flooding back. Even though from the safe and dry cocoon of the car it looks so far out there, it is for me a beacon of friendship, a reminder of what you can do when you put your mind to it, and a call to swim as often as I can.

Not all my friends are swimmers. My friend Diana isn't the biggest fan of cold water, although she is now dipping her toes in. We had always known one another but not enough that you'd call us friends. I don't know how our real friendship started but I've lost count of the number of cups of coffee I've had in her warm kitchen as her mini dachshunds run around. She is kindness personified, and in my earliest days in Donegal, when I was really struggling, her friendship kept me afloat. She's my third sister and I love her.

Moving house at any stage of life means having to dip your toe in the waters of new friendships. It's like the adult version of being the new kid in the school playground, hoping others will ask you to play or at the very least won't say no when you ask them can you play. This isn't always easy, especially when children are small and you are totally immersed in the world of mothering. I can say with hand on heart that my friends make me happy every single day. Being in their company makes my heart soar. I take great pleasure in their accomplishments and wins and I see how they are happy when I share the good things in my life too.

With so many things in a woman's life, friendships can go through different phases. Sometimes the friend you need or who needs you pops up when you least expect it. That's how it was with Geraldine. We met many years ago at Diana's house and I remember us chatting briefly that night. Geraldine lit up when she talked about her family and that night when Diana's husband Paul left us home, she skipped back into her house where her husband and children were sleeping.

Our paths didn't cross again for some time, and at that point Geraldine had suffered the most unbearable loss imaginable. Her whole family had died in a terrible car accident and Geraldine was the sole survivor. One Sunday morning, a couple of months after the accident, my swim buddies Jane and Liz had opted for a sheltered spot to swim in Moville as our usual spot at Shroove Beach was too choppy. Geraldine was there with her brother Henry and they had been swimming. I went over to speak to her. Geraldine told me that Henry would soon be leaving to go back to the UK and asked if I would go for a swim with her. We met the following week at Shroove. We haven't stopped swimming together since. Each week we check in with one another and catch up. Despite her immeasurable grief, she manages to do so much in our community and for her friends. I count her among my closest friends and our messages to one another always end with 'I love you'.

Of course moving your life elsewhere doesn't mean you lose track of old friends. Social media, WhatsApp video calls and a glass of wine over Zoom make it easier to stay in the lives of old friends. One of my oldest friends, Mary Calpin, and I try to meet up for a weekend once a year without husbands or children and we do not draw breath from talking to catch up.

Two old school friends, Antoinette and Mary, are also part of my inner circle. Because we go back so far with one another, we don't need to see one another every week to know we are always constant for one another. I count myself lucky to have good women in my life every single day.

On a Sunday morning I'm always to be found with two of them, Liz and Jane, at Shroove Beach. We've been swimming every Sunday now for years. We try to put in a bit of distance, although some days I'm convinced we really just go for the coffee and chat afterwards. We celebrate life's little ups and downs and plan our season of summer swims. We are one another's biggest cheer leaders. When Jane says she's going for a promotion at work, we provide the pep talk. When Liz launches her new business as a wedding celebrant, we whoop and holler and promise we'll bring her clients. When I tell them I'm writing this book, they tell me, 'Of course you are. We knew you would.' I laugh and tell them they know more than I did.

Women have these secret places in their hearts where they let in only the good women in their lives because they're the only ones who understand the feelings they're talking about. My mother and I have a shorthand for understanding these secret places. I will know before she speaks on the phone how she is as she will know with me.

In my almost half-century on this planet, I've learned that being open to new friendships has been one of the most rewarding experiences of my life. I've also learned that coming to enjoy and revel in the company of your own self is one of life's greatest gifts. I, who spent so long trying to escape the parts of myself I was let down by and disappointed in, know this very well. It has been a revelation that one of the most enjoyable things in my life is taking myself off to a quiet place and spending time with myself in the solitude of nature. I have learned to quieten down the noise of my anxiety and to listen to the beat of my own internal drum. These days when I get the kids out to school, the time I have to myself before school pick-up is like gold dust. I love nothing more than getting in my car, sometimes with Wyatt, playing my music loud and driving to the other side of Inishowen, to Dunaff or Leenan or Tullagh Strand and walking. There are days I won't meet a soul and my only company will be the birds wheeling down over the ocean. I appreciate this time alone and it's almost like it replenishes me to go back to the busyness of home and deal with all the comings and goings and commotion that come with two growing boys.

On these days I feel so grateful for the gift of my own company. I've learned to embrace that wild girl again – she's not really a girl any more, let's face it, but my mother's wish that the rough edges would somehow be smoothed with time never ever happened. I'm still tearing holes in clothes climbing fences and coming home muddied from not being able to resist a better look at the outer edges of a field.

I ran from my own nature for many years. It took me a long time to love myself like I would a friend. It sounds a bit cringey to say it like that, but if we can't love this sometimes stranger looking back at us in the mirror, then our capacity to love others is lessened, in my opinion. If you are running away from yourself, sit for a while, hold your own hand and even if you're not quite ready to embrace whole-heartedly all the parts of your messy self, make a promise to yourself to try because you deserve it and if you don't do it, nobody else will. Let the wild girl come back. She's there waiting for you to put your arm around her and give her a big hug. She'll let you know she was there all along, just hoping you'd remember her.

We are hardwired for connection. Connecting with the natural world brought me a comfort I could never have foreseen. Wanting to learn more about it, taking myself outdoors meant that another door was opening in my world. There's a little cove not far from where I live. We call it Port a Doras (literally 'port of the door') because as you approach this place along the coastal path, it looks like a doorway appears in the rock. When you walk through the rock, you find yourself in a natural amphitheatre. Surrounded by high walls to the rear and rocky pools when the tide goes out, it's the perfect place to while away some time trying to entice ancient crabs out of their dark holes.

Opening my heart to the rhythms of the wilder world has been a balm. On the days when I don't get out, I am restless. A longing opens up inside me that can only be satisfied by stepping into a tidal pool or walking across blanket bog. In its own way the natural world has been a beacon of light, shining brightly in dark times.

I have sometimes found myself driving along a road somewhere I don't know particularly well and looking out the window to see whitethorn hedges glowing at the edge of a green field. At times I long to disappear into the ripe green of it, to trail my fingers across the flowers.

At one time I sought out the wild places because here nobody could hear me cry. There was nobody to judge my rage. Often the only witnesses to my sobs were the trees or the cormorants. I want to say to anybody who is hurting: go to the wild places. Seek the solace of the riverbank or the woods and empty yourself of your tears. It's OK to cry and it's OK to let it all go. There's no judgement in nature. Some day you will go to the riverbank and you won't want to cry anymore. You'll want only to walk and observe the swallows sweep low to eat the flies that swarm over it in summer or watch the dance of the dragonflies. You'll walk a little at first and then a little further. You'll want to keep going and you'll keep coming back because of the feeling it has opened up inside you. You will revel in your own company and then one day you'll realise that you too are nature. You are part of this vast cycle of change and restoration.

There will come a day when you'll look out your kitchen window and see a sliver of blue in the sky and you'll sniff the scent of the earth after rain and you'll think to yourself that the housework can wait, there are more important things to do, to bear witness to. You will be pulled forth from your house by a force of longing to feel it, to touch it and to immerse yourself in it. In the quiet of it, you'll hear your own heartbeat and realise that this wonder is in you too.

The river that flows past our house on its journey to the ocean has become like a metaphor for me for how to move forward. I watch it most days. Some days I climb down the stone steps to feel it under my toes or to sit right next to it. In some places it's shallow and I can see the ancient stones buried there. In other places between the rocks, there are deceptively deep pools.

One day many years ago as I tried to retrieve something the boys had accidentally thrown into the river, I slipped and fell in. The hole was deep and the water was up past my thighs. On that day I was wearing a brand new pair of runners. Like a cartoon character, I slipped and slid, trying to keep my balance on a rock, before landing ungraciously in the river.

The boys, who were watching from the safety of the riverbank, laughed so hard they had to lie down. On seeing so much laughing, I could only laugh too. I could only see the ridiculousness of my fall. I walked out of the river dripping wet, the boys still laughing uncontrollably. I lay down beside them and all three of us laughed again. The river reminds me not to take myself so seriously.

There are huge boulders in the middle of it. Mostly the water never comes anywhere near the top of them, but in times of flood, they disappear altogether. I've often sat by the riverbank and watched how the water flows around one particularly large boulder. The only certainty is that the water will make its way to the sea. No obstruction, no matter how large, will stop it. Nothing will block its way and it will always find a way, not through but around.

I've been trying to move like that in the world. Instead of meeting intransigence or difficulties with my own hard-headedness, I've tried to let things flow. Some years ago I went on a retreat for women organised by the former professional surfer Easkey Britton, now a highly respected scientist. I heard about the retreat through a friend of Easkey's who I happened to be interviewing for a newspaper article. The retreat was called 'Move like Water' and it seemed to call me to attend. We used the medium of water to explore aspects of ourselves and our lives. We visited waterfalls, bathed in rivers and played in the surf before coming together in a circle again to chat about these experiences.

Now when I feel myself close up or clench in life situations, I try to think of the boulder in the middle of our river and how the water simply moves around it. I can't control so many of the things that happen in my life but I can control how I feel and how I react to them. Perhaps this is why I still go to watch the river. Its presence reminds me on a daily basis that life moves only forward and that I may as well go with the current as try to swim upriver against it.

On summer days when the flies swarm and the

dragonflies emerge, I find it tranquil to spend as much time as I can just observing it. We've been living beside it for over a decade now. Can I say that I always manage to go with the flow? No, is the answer. For so long I was intent on swimming up the river, against gravity, pushing myself.

One day not long ago, I had driven all day. I'd spent eight hours in the car and I felt like I was cooking slowly on a spit, the air conditioning doing nothing to keep me cool in the heat of the sun. As I arrived back home, I could see the big full moon in a still-bright sky sitting over the Foyle as if suspended on an invisible string. I called Geraldine to see if she wanted to join me for an impromptu swim. I needed to feel the coolness of the ocean against my skin that night. There's something about a full moon that makes me want to feel the elements all the more, even if it's only walking barefoot in the grass across the lawn and basking in the moon's glow.

The size of the tide at full moon is always a surprise. The water is full, the pull of the tide stronger. As I drove to the beach, I felt a strong sense of giving myself permission to be my full self. This feeling has eluded me at so many stages of my life. This full moon felt like a blessing, an invitation to join in a beautiful manifestation of nature and be myself. For so long I've felt not enough, stymied, harried, bereft and crazed. This urgency to be in the water was like a calling I had to answer. Perhaps this sounds a bit daft and maybe even a bit crazy. But something crystallised as I drove; I realised that all my searching was leading to this point. This point wasn't fixed. It wasn't having it all worked out. It was about freedom.

Bubbling up was this unbridled sense of freedom, to give total expression to how I was feeling, to feel the water on my skin and to reach out and feel all the feelings and to allow them to enter me and to let them go again. It was as if this moon was telling me I was not deficient. It was saying come as you are, you could not be more you.

I understood that I am not defined by the work I do, or by the babies I have or have never had. I'm not defined by my dress size, by my body or how much space I take up in a room. I'm not defined by other people's expectations of me or even by my own. I am defined by my heart and how much it loves and is loved back.

If you've come to the end of this journey with me, I hope that life's waves haven't bashed you too hard. If you're holding this book in your hand, please remember you're holding pieces of my heart. I am offering these pieces to say I'm still here, still swimming, still hoping, still loving and most of all still trying my best. I hope you are too.

CHAPTER 12

Find your own wild

Where did that wild girl go?
She got caught up with dinners and deadlines and her diary.
But one morning I caught sight of her in the woods,
her hair, flowing out behind her,
had snagged in a branch and a piece of it was caught there.
She was running fast and I only glimpsed her briefly
as she disappeared soundlessly behind a tree.
It was as if she was waiting for me to return
and then she could truly disappear.

W rite them on the table of your heart, the words that speak to your freedom. I have told my heart many stories but it sees through them all. The mind knows but the heart knows best. I am at an age where I can trust the heart too.

It's bitingly cold as I stand on the beach, my beach. I have it back after the hordes of summer have left. It's just me and the birds circling overhead. The cormorants on their rock, just out of reach of any swimmers, take up their usual perch. The sand is damp and I already know that it will be cold, like a morning in the desert. I slip out of my clothes easily and I can see my breath on the air. Cold but it will be colder still in the water. I walk into the tide, one step at a time. I don't slow my walk, although I'm not quite ready for the waves as they lash against my legs. My fingers trail the crest of the waves and I reach down and with handfuls of water splash the back of my neck to trigger the vagus nerve. It acts as a warning light to let the body know that more cold is coming. When I reach waist height, I push my arms in front of me and submerge myself, trying to keep my breath even. I breathe deeply, not allowing myself to panic or to let my breathing become shallow. I push my arms out in front, kicking my legs like a large frog – breast stroke is easiest on these days. I don't think I can put my face in the water until I have steadied myself. I flip onto my back and look out into the open Atlantic Ocean. I see the red Foyle buoy, which measures the water temperature and wave height. I didn't bother to check the temperature. What's the point?

It's somewhere north of freezing, but not that much. The greeny blue of the water in summer is replaced by the froth of waves in winter. I won't stay in long in this cold. I look at the lighthouse at the edge of the beach, sure and steady. How many years have I been looking at it, as if by watching it I will also be guided by its light to some direction within myself that always seemed quite out of reach? I try to imitate the water and to make myself one with it. I don't fight so much anymore. For so much of my life, I have been fighting against the tide – trying so hard for so long to have another baby. I can't honestly say if I wouldn't do the same things again, but with the benefit of hindsight I can see that life was going to unfold the way it was going to unfold and I should perhaps have tried not to push so hard against gravity or against nature. Maybe that's easy for me to say as a mother of two children. It's just my observation with the wisdom of some heartbreak and some years.

I look out to sea and then I see him; a large grey seal is solemnly and silently watching me. Maybe it's a she. Its sleek head is like wet rubber, its two eyes large in its beautiful face. It looks at me inquisitively as if begging the question: 'What are you?' For a moment I forget my cold self. I focus on the seal and its proximity. It dips below the surface and I watch for it to pop up again. Seconds later, it reappears, only this time it's much closer. The beach is still deserted. I call out to it in my best impersonation of a seal, somewhere between the bark of a dog and the noise I've heard seals in the zoo make. Is it my imagination or does the seal tip its head to one side as if trying to make out what I've said? I laugh out loud at the ridiculousness of this situation – me barking at the seal and the seal wondering what kind of creature is in its ocean. I lie on my back and kick and care not a fig for the rest of the world. In this place, I am my wild self, my true self. I am me and that is enough. It's always been enough.